# Cook
# Indonesian

# Cook Indonesian

**Agnes de Keijzer Brackman**

Photographs by
**K A Ang**

Kitchen-tested by
**Juliet Choo**
New Nation food columnist

TIMES BOOKS INTERNATIONAL
*Singapore • Kuala Lumpur*

First published in 1970
Reprinted 1974 by
Asia Pacific Press (Pte) Ltd, as
*The Art of Indonesian Cooking: The ABCs*
This revised and enlarged edition by
Times Books International,
an imprint of Times Editions Pte Ltd

© **1982 Times Editions Pte Ltd**
Times Centre
1 New Industrial Road
Singapore 1953

2nd Floor
Wisma Hong Leong Yamaha
50 Jalan Penchala
46050 Petaling Jaya
Selangor Darul Ehsan
Malaysia

Reprinted in 1991

Printed by Star Standard Industries (Pte) Ltd

ISBN 981 204 246 6

# Preface

I first wrote this book in 1969, after having spent many years in Southeast Asia, primarily Indonesia. At that time there were no books to speak of on the subject, at best a few desultory recipes tossed into general books on Asian cookery. The first edition of *The Art of Indonesian Cooking: The ABC's* was published in Singapore in 1970 — and sold out immediately. It went through several printings (much to my astonishment) and in 1974 a completely new edition was published in Singapore. That, too, went through several printings and by the end of the decade those printings were exhausted.

Over the years, several readers suggested a new edition with strong emphasis on photography (the original editions contained only a handful of pen-and-ink drawings, and no photographs). This new edition, *Cook Indonesian,* is an offshoot of those suggestions.

Interest in Indonesian cooking has changed radically over the past decade and more. When I first wrote this book Indonesian cookery was considered exotic, 'far out'. This is no longer the case, although it has yet to catch on to the extent that Japanese and Thai cooking has around the world in recent years. Before that, of course, the only Asian cookery most of the non-Asian world had ever heard about was Chinese and Indian. I believe that by the end of the eighties, Indonesian fare will take its rightful place as one of the world's great cuisines.

But the radical changes I mentioned above have already taken place, a harbinger of things to come. In 1969 it was difficult in the West to buy *tahu* (bean curd). Now, under the Japanese name of *tofu,* it is reasonably commonplace. In the United States, for example, there has been an astounding interest in *tempe* or fermented soybean, one of the world's great dishes. In the past few years hardly a month goes by that some food editor of a newspaper supplement or gourmet magazine does not carry a reference to *tempe.* I have seen such dishes as barbecued *tempe,* scrambled *tempe, tempe* burgers and *tempe* croquettes written about! There is even a mail order house in the United States that carries *tempe* kits and a *tempe* starter (ragi).

Ten years ago coconuts were a novelty item in Western food markets. Today they are commonplace in both Europe and America. And so, gradually, the ground swell in Indonesian cookery gains momentum. As the Indonesians like to say, **Selamat Makan!**

# Acknowledgements

The publishers wish to extend their thanks to all those who have involved themselves in *Cook Indonesian*, especially

Aw Pottery for the generous loan of their beautiful crockery;

Sarinah Jaya Singapore Pte. Ltd. at Singapore Handicrafts Centre;

Lee Geok Boi for her ever-helpful hints and resourcefulness;

Mr Anas, proprietor of Borobudur Arts and Crafts at Far East Shopping Centre, for his gentleness and goodwill;

and Madam Willemsen de Krijger, without whose abundant generosity in the loan of many personal items this book would never have come to be.

# Contents

# A Quick Reference

## Coconut milk

This ingredient is absolutely indispensable not only in Indonesian cooking, but virtually in all forms of South Asian cooking except for the Chinese.

Contrary to popular belief in the West, the refreshing, colourless liquid inside the coconut is not coconut milk. The preparation of coconut milk is not difficult, fortunately.

a) Purchase a fresh coconut and pierce one of the nut's eyes at the top. Use a sharp object such as a plain, down-to-earth screwdriver. Drain the liquid from the coconut. Children love it.

b) Now place the coconut in an oven, raise the temperature to 400° F (205° C) and heat for about twenty minutes. Cool the coconut. Break it open with a hammer.

c) Remove the meat from the shell with a dull paring knife. Remove the brown outer skin from the meat with a potato peeler.

d) Wash and grate the coconut meat. Add warm water as the recipe requires. For example, if a recipe calls for '½ cup coconut milk from ½ coconut', simply add ½ cup of warm water to ½ cup of grated coconut. 1 coconut yields 4 cups of grated coconut.

e) After the coconut 'milk' is cool, strain through a cheese cloth. (Squeeze coconut until all the milk is removed.) The milk is now ready for use.

## Tamarind juice

To prepare tamarind juice, place a piece of tamarind about the size of a domino in 2 tablespoons of lukewarm water, stir and stand for an hour. This is more than enough for all recipes requiring tamarind juice.

## Bean sprouts

To make fresh bean sprouts, place half a cup of mung beans (available in any Chinatown) in a dish. Add enough tepid water to barely cover them. Cover dish and place in dark cupboard. Check daily, add additional water to keep beans moist (but do not saturate). Beans should be ready in 3–4 days. Canned bean sprouts are also available in some supermarkets but the fresh variety is far superior.

## Chicken

Chicken dishes may be made a day before they are to be served, and placed in the refrigerator in a covered dish.

## Fish and shellfish

To save time, clean fish and shellfish in advance, salt lightly, and place in refrigerator until needed.

## Cabbage and string-bean dishes

These improve in flavour if made a day in advance of serving, and kept refrigerated.

## *Krupuk* and *rempeyeh*

Both can be fried the day before, thoroughly

cooled and kept in an airtight container until needed. They make excellent cocktail titbits.

## Relishes

Relishes and pickled dishes may be made several days in advance and stored for considerable periods in mason jars, tightly sealed and refrigerated.

## Grated coconut

Coconuts may be grated a week or more in advance and placed in either a pyrex dish or plastic freezing bag and kept in a deep freezer. Remove from the freezer several hours before needed.

## Keeping food warm

Dishes prepared the day before may be heated without burning by keeping the range at low heat while placing the dishes in the oven compartment. Dishes may be left in the oven for an hour or more while preparing the rice.

## Rice

For perfect rice, each grain separate and distinct, rinse American rice twice before cooking, and Asian-grown varieties several times. This washes away the small particles acquired during the milling process.

## Satay

Wrap ends of bamboo *satay* skewers with aluminium foil to prevent them from burning during a barbecue, Western style. An electric blender is a wonderful coconut grater and can also be used to prepare *saus kacang* or peanut sauce for *satay*.

## Fryer or boiler

Both terms refer to chickens which are 10–16 weeks old and weigh 1–3 pounds.

## Chilli

In the United States, as a result of Mexican influence, the word 'chilli' is often synonymous with chilli powder, which is stocked in every supermarket and grocery. Chilli powder is a mildly sharp and piquant mixture comprising paprika, cummin, oregano, salt, garlic and Cayenne pepper. The use of chilli powder in Indonesian cooking would result in a disaster.

## Soy sauce

In Indonesian cooking, sweet soy sauce is *kecap manis*. But dark soy sauce is *kecap asin* or salty soy sauce. There is a great difference between them. And in Indonesian cooking, sweet soy sauce is an absolute must. If, for example, you use Chinese dark soy sauce, which is very salty, and if it is used with salt added to the recipe we will have a monumental culinary disaster.

## Ingredients

For all the recipes in this book, use **ground** cloves, cummin, turmeric, coriander, *laos*, black pepper and grated nutmeg unless specified otherwise.

## Sambal ulek

Many of the recipes call for *sambal ulek*. The recipe for *sambal ulek* can be found on page 111.

# Where to Buy?

Many of the so-called 'exotic' ingredients used in the preparation of Indonesian dishes, such as shrimp paste and lemon grass leaves, are readily obtainable outside of Southeast Asia. The best source, as noted in the Introduction, is the nearest Indonesian embassy or consulate. They will be pleased that you show an interest in their food and will offer helpful hints as to where they buy their own ingredients locally. Generally, in the European world the best source is a Dutch firm, Conimex. Their address is:

Conimex
Baarn
Netherlands

If you live in Canada or the United States, there are three excellent importers at your disposal:

Mrs de Wildt
R.D. 3
Bangor, Pennsylvania 18013
U.S.A.

Merapi, Inc.
Oriental Food Products
139 White Street
Danbury, Connecticut 06810
U.S.A.

The Hollinda Co.
9544 Las Tunas Drive
Temple City
California 91780
U.S.A.

# Immeasurable Delight

This book is intended as a simplified guide through the labyrinth of a form of Asian cooking unknown generally in the West and in large parts of Asia, yet possessing a stature comparable to the renown of Chinese and French styles of cooking.

The reader should not accept each recipe in this volume as dogma. Cooking is an art, not a science. Ten cooks working with the same recipe will produce ten variations on a theme, some better and some worse. All a cookbook can really do is mark the guidelines and provide the reader with instructions for the preparation of specific dishes. The execution of the dish, however, is entirely in the hands of the cook. It is all a matter of personal taste. If a recipe calls for one teaspoon of ginger, the object of the author has been merely to convey to you that it is generally the amount used. Some persons may prefer slightly more ginger; others, slightly less.

Similarly, the meat you purchase on one occasion may not be as tender as on the next. Every cook knows this and also knows that this can affect the outcome of a dish.

While these observations may appear commonplace, I should like to stress again that the recipes in this book should not be taken literally. I have observed Indonesian cooks at work from the village to the palace level. They do not use graduated cups, scales and the paraphernalia commonplace in the machinery-cluttered modern kitchen. Intuitively, but actually as a result of trial and error, accompanied by an artistic flair, Indonesian cooks have put together some truly remarkable dishes by rule of thumb.

At all times, a recipe must be tasted to a happy conclusion. This is especially true when you are working with a variety of spices. A little more of this and less of that — do not be afraid to use your fingers. Keep tasting as you go along.

# For Squales

# Introduction : Points of Origin

For the gourmet, Indonesia, the Spice Islands of antiquity, may be likened to a kaleidoscope of Asian cookery. Indonesian food is an exciting blend of Moslem, Hindu and Buddhist influences. Expressed differently, it is a melding of Malay-Arab, Indian and Chinese culinary arts. In brilliant fashion, the Indonesians have subtly combined these contrasting influences and, primarily through the judicious use of the very spices which gave the islands their name, have developed a unique form of cookery.

The Indonesian centrepiece is the *rijsttafel*, in literal translation, 'rice table', a Dutch-minted phrase which has come into common usage throughout the islands. Once a rare epicurean experience, the *rijsttafel* can today be easily duplicated in the modern, Western-type kitchen. Essentially, a rice table consists of a mound of rice in an individual bowl, garnished with samplings of fifty or more peripheral dishes. The *rijsttafel* is ideal for a buffet, a sort of tropical, Asian smorgasbord.

The dishes composing the rice table range from familiar fishes in unfamiliar sauces to curried fowls, skewered cubes of lamb and pork, and vegetables skilfully blended with spices. The *rijsttafel* moved the late Miguel Covarrubias, the outstanding Mexican illustrator and author, to observe that 'the food that Balinese gourmets eat at festivals is as elaborate as any in the world'. Indeed, it is. As a brochure of the former Hotel des Indes, once known as the gateway to the Indies, noted, 'to be fully appreciated, the *rijsttafel* must be experienced — and the greater the experience, the greater the appreciation'.

Despite the increasing popularity of Oriental dishes in the Occident, relatively little has appeared in English on the art of Indonesian cooking. The purpose of this book is to help to fill the vacuum.

To appreciate the *rijsttafel,* one must appreciate its place of origin. To begin with, the islands of Indonesia are fashioned like a jade necklace, extending from the tip of Southeast Asia to the northern coastline of Australia. The archipelago is the world's largest, and it contains literally thousands of islands, or beads, to complete the metaphor. The names have a familiar ring: Sumatra, Java, Kalimantan (Borneo), Sulawesi (Celebes), Maluku (the Moluccas), and fabled Bali.

Westerners as well as Chinese and Indian travellers have been tempted by the epicurean delights of the islanders for centuries. In the thirteenth century, for example, the intrepid Marco Polo, after a twenty-year sojourn in Cathay, sailed for Europe by way of the island chain. His frail ship sailed among the islands for several months. An inveterate noter, he amassed a collection of recipes and spices. Indeed, he gave the archipelago the sobriquet 'Spice Islands'. In this region of the globe, he wrote, is 'obtained the greatest part of the spices that are distributed throughout the world'. Among them he listed pepper, nutmeg and clove. He apparently enjoyed Indonesian cooking. On Sumatra, for example, he found that people ate flesh 'clean and unclean'; among the clean, as today, buffalo and wild swine; among the unclean, the crocodile. In my part of the tropical world, the Amazon, we still eat lizard, the iguana; doubtless, Marco Polo would consider it 'unclean'.

The Genoese traveller was an accurate and descriptive writer. For example, imagine the Western reaction to his report of an Indonesian nut, which contains 'an edible substance that is sweet and pleasant to the taste, and white as milk'. The cavity of the pulp, he said, was filled with liquid — clear as water, cool, and better flavoured and more delicate than wine, or any other kind of drink whatever. The nut? The coconut, of course.

As for eating habits in the islands, he observed that the people produced 'no wheat, but lived on rice'. He also discovered that there were no grapes and, therefore, no wines in the archipelago. But sensibilities were reassured when he learned of a species of tree resembling the date-bearing palm, from which the Indonesians procured 'an excellent beverage'. He then proceeded to give the recipe for palm wine.

Things have not changed that much since then in the Indonesian kitchen. Today, as yesterday, the people still 'live on rice'. In the words of an Indonesian government authority, 'A meal is not a meal unless there is rice.' But rice is only the plinth upon which the *rijsttafel* is constructed. All told, there are 1,000 Indonesian recipes, more or less; invariably, rice is at the base of all of them.

This brings us back to the question of just precisely what is a *rijsttafel*? Among foreigners, in Indonesia, the big rice table has become a Sunday ritual. Properly served in the old days, the drama develops like this. A headwaiter approaches the table carrying a huge bowl of steaming white rice, followed by an Indian file of as many as thirty waiters, each bearing a deep bowl or oval platter, or sometimes a lazy susan. Each plate and/or compartment contains a different dish.

First you build a small mound of rice in the centre of your bowl. Then, as each waiter files by, you take a helping from his tray. The mound of food, which starts like a knoll, gradually grows into a veritable mountain. As the last waiter moves to the adjoining table to repeat the process (much to your relief), the dining commences.

There is no formal procedure in putting together a rice bowl. Some people try to keep each sample of food separate (a hopeless task); others mix everything together with an air of carefree abandon, and top the dish with peanut sauce. In any event, each spoonful — the *rijsttafel* is eaten primarily with a spoon and fork, but no knife — provides a unique taste sensation. Although most Indonesians are nominally Moslem and prefer either water or a soft drink with their meal, a tall, frosty glass of beer is highly recommended. Indeed, it is mandatory.

In these hurried days, the *rijsttafel* has devolved into a buffet. Most of Indonesia's new, modern hotels serve it in this manner. I suppose self-service is egalitarian, in tune with the age. It certainly is less elegant, although I must concede that at village feasts, especially in the outer islands, the buffet style reigns supreme.

The unique character of the *rijsttafel* is not born solely of variety. If it were merely a question of preparing different kinds of dishes, a rice table would simply be a super French *hors d'oeuvres* or Italian *antipasto*. But the portions in a *rijsttafel* are far more generous, and a couple of dishes with rice could easily constitute a full meal.

Perhaps in no other form of cooking is there such a prolific use of spices, in a variety of combinations with results ranging from fiery to sweet and mild. In some ways, Indonesian cooking is like opening a spice safe. If you know the proper combination, the door swings open easily.

One piece of Western nonsense must be dispensed with immediately. Among the uninitiated, the mistaken notion arises that spices necessarily denote 'hot' food. That may be the case, but it is not necessarily true. Some spices are decidedly sweet, others are simply aromatic; some are mild and, of course, others unforgettably searing.

Spices of course have been employed in the kitchen since the first camp-fire. The Aztecs and the Egyptians used them with sophistication. Both the Bible and the Koran have references to them. Nowhere, however, is there a more natural spice chamber than in the islands of Indonesia, where people have cultivated spice gardens since time immemorial. Centuries of usage have refined the employment of spices in their culinary art to the point of perfection.

Let us briefly examine some of the more familiar spices, which we shall be using in the pages ahead.

Perhaps the best known, and most popular spice, is the pepper vine, a perennial climbing shrub which is widely cultivated in southern Sumatra, in Kalimantan (Borneo) and on the islands of Bangka and Billiton, situated in the Java-Singapore-Sumatra triangle. Most cooks distinguish between black and white pepper. Black pepper is simply unripened, dried pepper. White pepper is the familiar black pepper, but unhulled. There is still another pepper: the red variety, also green sometimes. But, oddly enough, red pepper is unrelated to the pepper vine. It is generally known as chilli and the dried form as Cayenne pepper after the capital of French Guiana which adjoins my native Surinam.

It is an incendiary spice. In fact, our South American variety is hotter than the Southeast Asian, and I have confirmed this by trying it out on Achenese friends. They boast about their ability to consume flaming hot food.

Invariably, the hotter the climate, the hotter is the food. This is a generally accepted axiom. Hot food is supposed to ventilate the body; it acts as a sort of air-conditioner. There are exceptions to the axiom, however. Inexplicably, Korean food is hot.

About a decade ago, the National Geographic Society in the United States sent two travellers, Helen and Frank Schreider, to Indonesia. Their first Indonesian meal with an Indonesian family was memorable. They wrote:

'We want you to try Indonesian food,' our host said, heaping our plates with steaming *satay,* a miniature kebab; flaky chips of *krupuk,* ground shrimp; *gado-gado,* a vegetable dish with peanut sauce; and mounds of boiled, white rice.
'The food is not spicy enough,' she advised us. 'You must add your own *sambal,* our Indonesian pepper sauce.'
Both Helen and I like hot food, and I used the *sambal* liberally. The result was as explosive as the eruption of Krakatoa, Indonesia's famous volcano. Blinded by tears, I groped for the tea in a frantic effort to put out the fire.

This, alas, is the usual introduction to hot spices. But then there are the sweet and aromatic spices such as cinnamon, a member of the laurel family. Some of the Indonesian trees which still yield an abundance of the bark from which cinnamon is processed are older than the American and French Revolutions. My husband contends, however, that the cinnamon of Vietnam rivals that of Java. Another sweet or mild spice closely related to cinnamon is cassia. And still another is the nutmeg, the evergreen which grows wild in Maluku (the Moluccas) and whose outer covering is used in the kitchen under the name of mace. It may seem out of place to write of evergreens in the tropics, but they are there.

Another spice-producing evergreen is the clove tree. It sometimes grows more than 9.1 metres (30 feet) in height; at least it does on Ambon. It has clusters of yellow-pink flowers which are picked when the colour turns brick-red. Indonesians are particularly fond of the nail-shaped cloves.

Incidentally, the aroma of cloves hangs heavy over most of Indonesia, like a smog, but a far more pleasant smog than that of London or Los Angeles. I am not exaggerating about this smog business, and the cause is relatively understandable. Indonesians delight in mixing cloves in their cigarette tobacco. Every time an Indonesian lights up (and there are almost one hundred million chain-smokers in the islands), the cigarette smoke gives off an aroma of cloves. Imagine hundreds of millions of tiny rolls of paper, cloves and tobacco going up in smoke daily! The spice smog is especially noticeable in the *desa* or village areas, away from the cities and their ubiquitous combustible engines.

Another spice frequently used in Indonesian cooking which is far from hot is ginger. We used to grow ginger in our garden in Java not simply for the ginger, which is taken from the bulbous root, but for the lovely purplish flowers they produce. Closely related to ginger is turmeric, which is native to Indonesia and which is indispensable in Indian and Pakistani cooking. Its colour and taste vary from place to place throughout southern Asia. Only the turmeric of Bengal can match that of Indonesia. Turmeric, of course, is basic in the preparation of curry. Indeed, many of the other spices which go to make curry are found in the Spice Islands, including cardamom (usually misspelt as 'cardamon') and cummin, which has a slightly bitter (not hot) taste and is used in the West for pickling and sausage making.

This brief review of spices would be incomplete without another favourite found in the Indonesian kitchen: coriander. The seeds are crushed, thereby producing one of the most fragrant of all spices. Coriander leaves are often used for curries. The famous Chinese parsley is simply coriander leaves. According to legend, coriander has the power of a love potion. I suspect it is widely used in the islands as an aphrodisiac.

Lastly, the Indonesian spice shelf includes various leaves such as the *salam,* or bay or laurel leaf, which has the taste of bitter almonds, and *sereh* or lemon grass. In Indonesia, *sereh* is used either dry or fresh.

I have run through the gamut of the more popular Indonesian spices because of the dramatic role they play in the preparation of a *rijsttafel.*

Obviously, the preparation of a rice table can be a major undertaking. However, the recipes in this book have been especially selected, so that small *rijsttafels* or buffets may be easily prepared as zestful substitutes for otherwise common dishes. The ingredients mentioned in the recipes to follow are, of course, readily obtainable in Southeast Asia. In Australia, Japan or the West, the suggestion is simply to write to the local Indonesian embassy and inquire as to their source of raw materials. Indonesian missions abroad invariably serve Indonesian food and they usually have the address of a local distributor who, more often than not, imports his supplies from Holland. However, you will find that it is not difficult to obtain Indonesian ingredients in Britain, America or elsewhere.

As you will notice later on, unlike most Chinese, Western and Indian cookbooks, the recipes which follow do not specifically suggest how many people may be served from one dish. The reason is that Indonesian dinners consist of many dishes. As a general rule, four persons may eat well if the *rijsttafel* consists of rice, one chicken, one satay dish and one vegetable dish. For each additional couple add one dish. Of course after a while you may wish to make larger portions of some dishes and smaller ones of others. But each recipe in this book is designed to complete a simple, easily prepared rice table of rice plus three other dishes. Of course, with rice, when you have Asians at dinner, the amount consumed is double or triple that when only Westerners are seated at the table. But the Asians offset this by not eating much meat or fish. The Occidentals go skimpy on the rice and fill their bowls generously with everything else in sight.

I keep referring to the rice table as Indonesian, which it is. But nobody really knows of its origin, that is, how it came about. Marco Polo, for example, does not touch on the subject. Some historians have speculated (as historians are wont to do) that the *rijsttafel*, as the Indonesians know it today, did not exist in their time. Significantly, for that matter, Sir Stamford Raffles, the founder of Singapore, administrator, botanist and historian extraordinary, did not mention it in his two-volume history of Java. The probability, however, is that his notes about and recipes from the Indonesian kitchen were lost at sea, together with his collection of flora and fauna, when one of his ships foundered in a monsoon off the west coast of Sumatra. Speculation is irresistible.

The popular authoress, Emily Hahn, argues that the rice table is a relatively recent development dating from about the start of the last century. She contends that the colonizing Dutch avoided rice when they first settled in the East Indies. With characteristic conservativeness, the Hollanders are supposed to have approached Indonesian food with a degree of temerity, first tasting one dish, then sampling another. The Dutch were indecisive and simply added one dish to another over the centuries until the full *rijsttafel* emerged. This story has a touch of the Charles Lamb ring to it. Miss Hahn, however, provides some evidence that the *rijsttafel* was full blown by the time of the Napoleonic Wars, when Raffles was the Lieutenant-Governor of Java. She quotes from a letter written by Victor Ido van de Wall in 1812, which describes a Dutch breakfast in those days as consisting of 'warm rice, curry, fish, beefsteak, *dendeng* (dried meat), Macassar fish, peppers, greens (and) roast chicken, lavishly washed down with red wine, beer, Madeira, Rhine wine, brandy and seltzer water'. A Lucullian meal, indeed. The Dutch are justly famous for their appetites. But what could conceivably have constituted lunch or dinner after a breakfast of those dimensions? Whatever the case, the de Wall description has the ear-marks of today's rice table.

No matter what the origins of Indonesian cookery — from Hindu invaders, Arab traders, Chinese settlers or Dutch colonizers — the art of Indonesian cooking holds the prospect of new horizons for the gourmet. It is a gustatory challenge worth accepting.


Agnes de K. Brackman
Brookfield Center
Connecticut, USA
1982

# Rice : The Main Prop

Rice requires little introduction. *Oryza sativa linn* is more than the Asian staff of life: it is a gift of the gods. At least it is on Java, where it is revered as the offspring of Dwie Srie, a goddess. No festival in Indonesia is complete without rice in some form. On some islands, rice dolls are fashioned from the stalk of the plant and given as good-luck pieces to brides and pregnant women; I once sent my sister-in-law a rice doll from Bali and apparently it worked (she already has three children). This relationship between rice and fecundity, by the way, is not merely a quaint bit of Asian folklore. In the West, no church wedding is complete without a handful of rice thrown at the retreating bride and groom.

The place of origin of rice is open to considerable speculation, although the trend among botanists is to cite Southeast Asia as the native habitat. Here, at least, there is no doubt that rice grows in a wild state. From Southeast Asia, it is presumed to have travelled westward into India, Persia, Egypt, Greece and Rome, and northward into China, Korea and Japan. In the West, rice is relatively a late development; the Bible does not mention it. We do know, however, that in 1685, it was introduced into South Carolina. Today the United States is a leading rice producer and exporter, but still not a consumer.

Rice varies in size and taste from region to region. It is a matter of personal preference, but I prefer the Indonesian, Burmese, Vietnamese and South Chinese varieties. In Indonesia a superb rice is grown on the Krawang delta situated between Jakarta and Ciribon, along the northern coastline of Java. Among the better kinds of rice must be listed the long-grain, white variety, grown in the American South, usually in Arkansas, Louisiana or the Carolinas.

Unfortunately, many people are easily terrified at the thought of cooking rice. Too often, professionals (restaurant cooks), semi-professionals (housewives) and amateur chefs concoct something termed 'rice' but more easily identified as bookbinder's paste. How often, even in a euphemistically characterized 'Chinese' restaurant, have you been served soggy, sticky, glutinous rice with each grain clinging desperately to the other so that the end product is an unrecognizable, unappetizing white mass of mush? Properly prepared, each grain of rice should stand by itself, separate and distinct, like tiny grains of sand on a beach. Rice cookery would seem to compare with the interminable conflict between man and the mob.

The truth, however, is that rice is relatively simple to cook. There are a few basic rules that any child can follow. Kitty (Cathay), our daughter, can cook rice without difficulty and she has been doing so since she was nine. Since rice is the plinth of the Asian meal — whether Indonesian, Chinese or Sri Lankan — no Oriental epicurean edifice can be erected without it. Thus, the mastery of rice cookery is mandatory.

My suggestion to the beginner is to disregard completely the invariably misleading instructions found on packaged rice. It is inexplicable why these firms persist in prescribing mucilage recipes for rice recipes. Perhaps more perplexing is why housewives persist in pursuing instructions which they know by experience simply will not work.

The beginner should also bear in mind several basic pointers. Never use too large a pot for cooking rice and never fill the pot more than one-third full with uncooked rice. If you must use an aluminium pot, carefully observe the special instructions for it.

The basic cause of most trouble in rice cookery is the pot. In China, India and Pakistan, copper and brass pots are preferred; in Indonesia and most of Southeast Asia, the iron pot. In some places, a trivet is used for good measure, for example in South America. These reasons will be explained shortly. The important point in this brief introduction to rice is that it is a great dish when properly made and that it can be easily prepared.

Next time you open a packet of rice, remember that 3000 million people eat rice every day at every meal — and apparently they do not encounter too much trouble in its preparation. No, they do not tire of it, no more than a Westerner tires of eating wheat in one form or another every day at almost every meal during his life.

## COOKING RICE

The selection of the type and size of the pot or saucepan is the critical factor in the preparation of rice. The pot should be of thick metal: iron, copper or an alloy of brass and copper. The decisive element is the bottom, which is the surface exposed to the fire. If the bottom is made from thick or heavy metal, it shields the rice from burning and singeing — a common failure.

In the West, the most common culinary metal is aluminium. This could mean disaster in cooking rice. The walls of an aluminium pot are too thin and the heat penetrates intensely. But this problem is easily surmounted. The secret is to place an old-fashioned potato baker or cookie sheet over the range burner and then place the aluminium pot on top of it. The addition of this slim piece of extra metal between the flame and the bottom of the aluminium pot shields the bottom of the pot and reduces the heat tremendously. At home, in the interior of jungle-cloaked Surinam, which abuts on the Amazon and where aluminium pots are the fashion (Surinam has the world's largest reserve of bauxite, the red-rich loam from which aluminium

is processed), my mother places a cast-iron trivet between the flame and the aluminium pot.

Using the potato baker, cookie sheet or trivet necessitates an additional fifteen minutes of cooking. But the results are infallible. Such a cooking device, known as the 'flame tamer' or 'flame master', is available in any American department store.

In addition to the problem of selecting the correct utensil, another important factor in the preparation of rice — often overlooked — is the size of the pot. Too large a pot should be avoided. The uncooked rice should fill only one-third the area of the pot. The cooked rice will fill the vacant area as it expands during the cooking process.

Having selected the correct pot, put 2 cups of rice in the pot and wash twice under cold tap water. Now drain and add 2½ cups of cold water. Stir well with a fork and cover tightly. Place the pot over low heat and cook for about 45 minutes. Then stir once with a fork, replace cover and cook another 15 minutes. The moisture should now be completely absorbed by the grains.

A last tip: it is always better to have less water than too much. If the rice is not cooked enough at the end of the specified cooking time you can always sprinkle or gently add in more water and cook the rice a little longer. Too much water, however, results in a soggy mass of mucilaginous quality.

One pound (450 g) of rice, properly cooked, should make four to six servings, accompanied by Indonesian side-dishes.

See the recipe for Plain White Rice for an alternative method. Either method may be used with confidence.

# Nasi Putih (Plain White Rice)

2 cups long-grain rice
2½ cups water

Wash rice twice under cold tap water. Drain. Place in saucepan and add 2½ cups of cold water. Bring to the boil and simmer uncovered until all water has been absorbed.

Cover saucepan, lower heat and cook for a further 15 minutes.

# Nasi Guri (Fragrant Rice)

2 cups long-grain rice
2½ cups coconut milk from
  1 coconut
2 *salam* leaves
2 teaspoons salt
1 large onion, sliced
3 tablespoons margarine *or* vegetable oil
1 small cucumber
2 eggs
1 tablespoon milk
spicy coconut balls

Basically the method of preparation is the same as that of plain white rice but with this difference: after washing and draining rice substitute coconut milk for the usual 2½ cups of cold water. Add *salam* leaves and salt.

While rice is cooking prepare these 4 garnishes:
1. Fry the sliced onion in oil until brown and crispy.
2. Peel the cucumber and slice thinly.
3. Make an omelette with the eggs, using milk and a pinch of salt. Cut the omelette into strips.
4. Make spicy coconut balls. (see recipe on page 101).

After rice is cooked, place in an oval platter and garnish with the preceding items. Serve. Nasi Guri is prepared in Indonesia on special occasions like festivals, Islamic holidays, birthdays and weddings.

# Nasi Ayam (Chicken and Rice)

1 quartered chicken, about
   2½ lb (1¼ kg)
2½ tablespoons salt
1 *salam* leaf
1 cinnamon stick
3 cups coconut milk from
   1 coconut
2 cups long-grain rice

Wash and clean chicken thoroughly. Place in a heavy saucepan and add salt, *salam* leaf, cinnamon stick and 2 cups coconut milk. Cover tightly and cook over medium heat for about 30 minutes.

Remove chicken from stock. Add remainder of coconut milk to stock, stir and measure out 2½ cups of the liquid.

Wash rice twice with cold tap water, drain completely, add the liquid and cook rice.

Add chicken after rice has cooked a half-hour, then steam for an additional 15 minutes or until done.

When serving bury the chicken in the rice.

# Nasi Kebuli (Fragrant Rice and Chicken)

*illustrated on page 26*

2 medium onions, sliced
1 quartered chicken, about 2½ lb (1¼ kg)
1 teaspoon lemon grass
½ teaspoon *laos*
½ teaspoon coriander
3 lime leaves
2 cloves garlic, chopped
1 tablespoon salt
3 tablespoons vegetable oil
2 cups long-grain rice
pinch of nutmeg
pinch of ginger
4 peppercorns
2 pieces mace

Fry sliced onions in oil until a medium brown. Set aside.

Wash and clean chicken. Place in a heavy saucepan. Add lemon grass, *laos*, coriander, lime leaves, garlic, salt and 2 cups water. Cover tightly and cook chicken until tender.

Remove chicken from stock, reserving it for later use, and fry chicken in oil until golden brown.

Cook the rice in 2½ cups of chicken stock following the usual procedure but adding nutmeg, ginger, peppercorns and mace with the stock.

Place the cooked rice in a large platter with the aromatic chicken along the edges.

Sprinkle rice with fried onions. Serve.

# Nasi Kuning (Yellow Rice)

2 cups long-grain rice
2½ cups coconut milk from
   1 coconut
1 teaspoon turmeric
½ teaspoon coriander
1 *salam* leaf
2 cloves garlic, chopped
2 teaspoons salt
1 large onion, sliced
1 tablespoon vegetable oil
1 medium cucumber, peeled
  and cut into long strips

After rice has been washed and drained add coconut milk, turmeric, coriander, *salam* leaf, garlic and salt. Cook, covered tightly, over medium heat.

Meanwhile fry the sliced onion in oil.

Garnish rice with the fried onion and sliced cucumber. Serve.

# Nasi Goreng (Fried Rice, Indonesian Style)

2 cups long-grain rice
2 teaspoons salt
1 chicken breast, diced
2 tablespoons margarine *or* vegetable oil
2 large onions, sliced
2 cloves garlic, chopped
½ teaspoon coriander
½ teaspoon *laos*
sliver of shrimp paste
1 red chilli, crushed
2 tablespoons sweet soy sauce
1 cup cooked shrimps
1 fried egg (optional)

Cook rice in the usual manner but remember to add salt with the 2½ cups of water. After rice is cooked, set aside until sufficiently cool.

Fry diced chicken in margarine or oil until light brown. Add sliced onions and sauté with chicken until onion browns.

Lower heat and add chopped garlic, coriander, *laos* and shrimp paste. Stir well and add crushed red chilli. Fry the combination for about 1 minute. Then add soy sauce and shrimps, mixing thoroughly. Finally add the pre-cooked rice. Maintain a low steady heat, stir constantly until rice turns light brown.

In Indonesia, Nasi Goreng Istimewa (Fried Rice Special) is fried rice topped with a fried egg.

*Note:* Though chicken and shrimp are used in this recipe, any kind of meat or fish will do as well, as long as it is properly diced.

Ingredients basic to Indonesian cooking:

| | | | | | | | |
|---|---|---|---|---|---|---|---|
| 1 | garlic | 4 | lime leaves | 7 | laos | 10 | gula Jawa | 13 | tamarind | 16 | candlenuts |
| 2 | shallots | 5 | ginger | 8 | lemon grass | 11 | nutmeg | 14 | turmeric | 17 | black peppercorns |
| 3 | chillies | 6 | dried chillies | 9 | mace | 12 | cummin | 15 | coriander | 18 | cloves |

Nasi Kebuli (p. 23) and Rempah Kelapa (p. 101)

Sambal Goreng Udang Kering (p. 37)

Bebotok Kepiting Jawa (p. 39)

# Nasi Ulam (Rice and Spice)

2 cups long-grain rice
1 small onion, chopped
2 cloves garlic, chopped
2 tablespoons vegetable oil
pinch of cummin
1 teaspoon coriander
½ red chilli, crushed
½ teaspoon lemon grass
2 teaspoons salt
2 lime leaves
¼ roll shrimp paste
2½ cups coconut milk from 1 coconut

Wash rice twice in cold tap water, drain and set aside.

Sauté chopped onion and garlic in oil. Add cummin, coriander, crushed red chilli, lemon grass and salt. Stir well.

Now add in the rice and stir continuously until thoroughly mixed with spicy ingredients. Add lime leaves and shrimp paste.

Cook the mixture in coconut milk according to the directions for making plain white rice.

This dish may be garnished with fried onion, peeled and sliced cucumber, an egg omelette cut into strips, or a handful of fried peanuts.

# Lontong (Rice in Banana Leaves)

2 cups long-grain rice
banana leaves

Wash rice twice and drain. Fill into banana leaves and fold in oblong pieces, fastening with toothpicks. Add 10 cups of water initially.

Boil for about 3 hours. It may be necessary to add more water during this period.

OR

1 cup long-grain rice
banana leaves

Wash rice twice, add 2 cups of water and boil rice until soft.

Place in banana leaves, roll into oblongs and fasten with toothpicks. Boil for about 1 hour.

Chill, slice and serve. Lontong is a good accompaniment for dishes like Gado-gado or a *sambal*.

*Note:* In the West or wherever banana leaves are hard to come by, use aluminium foil or corn husks as wrappers.

# Fish and Other Seafood

Indonesia is the largest archipelago in the world, embracing 1,903,650 square kilometres of islands and seas. Its waters abound in seafood: fishes, shrimp, molluscs, turtles and other forms of sea life. As elsewhere in Southeast Asia, fish and shrimp are served either grilled, roasted or sautéed in spicy sauces. They are also ground fine, dried on mats in the sun, mixed with sea-water, permitted to ferment and then made into an acrid, pungent, rich paste. In Indonesia this paste is called *trassi* and is found in almost every Indonesian dish. It can either be inexpensively purchased from importers in the Western world or anchovy paste may be used as a substitute. In Indonesia the odour of *trassi* permeates the kitchen.

'I was to find this a daily smell, punctual and inevitable as the morning smell of coffee at home,' the late Colin McPhee, the musicologist and former Balinese resident, wrote. 'It was unbelievably putrid. An amount the size of a pea was more than enough to flavour a dish. It gave a racy, briny tang to the food, and I soon found myself craving it as an animal craves salt.'

Some of the fishes of Indonesia are exotic but many of them are familiar on the Chinese or Western dinner table — sardines, anchovies, summer flounder (fluke), halibut, bonito, mackerel and school tuna. They may be found in many of the Indonesian ports which stud the coastline. Each seaside village boasts a *pasar ikan* or fish market of its own. As soon as the graceful, sea-going prau with enormous eyes painted on their port and starboard bow (so that the vessel can 'see' where she is sailing) arrives in a harbour, the fish are unloaded and briskly sold. Often, street-hawkers will buy up the catch, string the fish through the gills along a bamboo pole and then trudge down the nearest dusty roads for the inland villages, shouting their wares on the way. Small Chinese tricycles will

also suddenly appear on the scene and buy up basketfuls of fish, rushing them to the big towns.

Perhaps the pièce de résistance among Indonesian salt-water catches is the *kakap,* a giant sea perch and member of the marine bass family which tastes like fillet of sole — only better. In restaurants and hotels, *kakap à la meuniere* is a favourite on the menu. The *kakap* inhabits the muddy coastline and is sometimes taken in big, fresh-water rivers such as the Solo which courses through Central Java. Another Indonesian favourite is the *gurami*. It is to the island's fresh-water fishes what *kakap* is to the salt-water varieties. Every village has its *gurami* pond; curried or sautéed in spices, *gurami* is an especially fine dish. No rice table is complete without one fish course and *kakap* or gurami usually fills the bill; in the West, porgy and sea bass are ideal substitutes.

At Bagangsiapiapi, on the east coast of Sumatra, Indonesia once boasted the largest fishing port in the world, and the waters of eastern Indonesia are still a fisherman's paradise. East of the imaginary Wallace line, which flows through the Macassar Strait, and which divides the flora and fauna of Indonesia between Asia and Oceania, the islands lose their Asian characteristics and assume the appearance of the South Sea islands of the Joseph Conrad and Robert Louis Stevenson epics. The Macassar Strait and the waters around Sulawesi, Banda and Maluku are favourite haunts of the fork-tail fishes: bonito, tuna and mackerel.

Bonito, called *tongkol* or *jakalong,* abound in eastern Indonesia. They appear in schools and are often caught on chicken feather lures. On the picturesque island of Ambon, bonito is served at breakfast with rice and spices — a distant cry from bacon and eggs. Tuna is also plentiful. The Indonesians call them *abu-abu* (ash-ash), or *tonny,* a derivative of the Dutch word *tonijn.* Mackerel is another familiar fish and can be found anywhere from the Sangir Talaud islands south of the Philippines to the coast of east Java. Cooked in coconut or peanut oil, the mackerel or *banjar* (as the Javanese call it) is an epicurean treat.

Although the flat-fishes such as the fluke and flounder enjoy immense popularity in the West, the Indonesians tend to treat them with disdain, perhaps because of their unusual appearance. The largest and most frequently caught flat-fish in the islands is the *langkau,* a relative of halibut of the Grand Banks off Canada's eastern coast. Another familiar fish, introduced with considerable success by the Chinese, is the carp. The Chinese must have brought with them some prize specimens from Cathay. The finest I have ever seen was in a pond at the home of an Indonesian of Chinese ancestry in Celebes, or Sulawesi as the Indonesians now call the octopus-shaped island. In Indonesia, the carp is appropriately called *ikan emas* or gold fish, although carp lose their gold colouring as they mature. In west Java, in the hilly country beyond Bogor, there are innumerable *ikan emas* ponds, and pedlars of *ikan emas* take their wares from town to town.

The waters of Indonesia have other familiar fishes, such as the *ikan kakaktua* (named after the parrot-like *kakaktua* bird) which is similar to our black-fish. It has a strong beak and a mouth rimmed with a full set of teeth. Then there is the sailfish, which the Indonesians call similarly: *ikan* (fish) *lajar* (sail). Another is the *bandeng* which is a cross between the salmon and a distant cousin of the herring; smoked, *bandeng* is one of the great dishes of the world. Other popular Indonesian fishes, invariably cooked in spices, are the *kuro,* which reminds me of a barracuda, and the *lajang,* which has the appearance of a Caribbean jack-fish.

A survey of Indonesia's table fishes would be incomplete without a passing mention of the small fishes which are so popular in the islands, such as *ikan teri* or anchovy, and the *lemuru* or sardine. Dried and salted, they are used to garnish various dishes. On the Western-type cocktail circuit, dried *ikan teri* in particular makes a tasty titbit, especially with a gimlet. (Note: A proper gimlet is four parts gin and one part lemon squash, not lemon juice. In recent years, alas, the British-invented gimlet has lost its popularity in Southeast Asia and, as I discovered on my last trip, even in Kuala Lumpur, Singapore, and the northern Bornean states, the martini has become increasingly fashionable. I found this rather disappointing since a martini invariably tastes better before a crackling log fire with deep snow on the ground outside and icy winds buffeting the house. Be that as it may.)

Of course, there are other forms of seafood used in the Indonesian kitchen. Giant shrimps, better known as prawns, are in great abundance. They are not only made into paste, but are often fried in coconut oil with spices. Shrimps are also skewered, *satay*-style. In the old Kota section of Jakarta, near the Dutch drawbridges and forts built 300 years ago, a wide variety of shellfish and giant sea turtles are available. This is the area known as *Pasar Ikan,* a kind of Fulton fish market, which is a must for anyone interested in Indonesian cookery.

Squid and tiny octopus are also available, and they are kitchen favourites in the islands. In the following section, however, I have omitted the quaint delicacies such as octopus. By experience, I have found that Westerners tend to avoid them and, in any event, they are not generally available in most Western fish markets, Italian and Spanish markets excepted. Moreover, Europeans and Americans invariably eat almost the same kind of fish as the Indonesians, give or take a fin here or there. Accordingly, I have kept to the popular fishes, such as porgy (scup), sea bass, carp, cod, mackerel, bonito and smelt. For a really big fish, the striped bass, cooked in soy sauce, is a masterpiece. At a Christmas party some years ago we featured a striped bass which my husband, an incurable fisherman, caught off Montauk Point, Long Island, opposite our Connecticut shore-line. It proved very successful.

# Ikan Bali (Bali Fish)

*illustrated on page 47*

1 fish, about 1½-2 lb (650-900 g) dressed weight,
  preferably porgy *or* sea bass *or* mackerel
1 teaspoon salt
oil for deep-frying
2 tablespoons margarine *or* vegetable oil
2 small onions, sliced
1 teaspoon *sambal ulek*
½ teaspoon *laos*
½ teaspoon lemon grass
3 tablespoons tamarind juice
pinch of ground ginger
1 teaspoon brown sugar
1 tablespoon sweet soy sauce

Cut fish into serving portions and rub salt all over. Deep-fry and drain on absorbent paper.

Heat oil and sauté sliced onions until lightly brown. Add *sambal ulek*, *laos*, lemon grass, tamarind juice, ginger, brown sugar and soy sauce. Heat thoroughly.

Place fried fish in deep serving dish and pour sauce over it. Serve.

# Ikan Kecap (Soy Fish)

1 whole fish, about 1-1½ lb (450-650 g)
  dressed weight, preferably porgy *or* sea
  bass *or* carp
1 teaspoon salt
2 tablespoons vegetable oil
2 cloves garlic, chopped coarsely
1 large onion, chopped coarsely
1 teaspoon *sambal ulek*
2 tablespoons sweet soy sauce
pinch of ground ginger
½ teaspoon *laos*
1 *salam* leaf
1 tablespoon tamarind juice

Rub fish all over with salt. Set aside.

Heat oil and sauté garlic and onion until lightly brown. Add fish and lower heat. Then add *sambal ulek*, soy sauce, ginger, *laos* and *salam* leaf and baste repeatedly.

Cover tightly and cook over very low heat for about 20 minutes. Baste continuously. Water may be added to prevent fish from adhering to pan.

Add tamarind juice 5 minutes before removing from fire. Serve immediately.

*Note:* This recipe can be used for a large fish such as a striped bass of 12 lb (6 kg). Spices, however, must be adjusted according to taste and the size of the catch.

# Ikan Panggang (Barbecue Fish)

1 whole fish, about 1½-2 lb (650-900 g)
  dressed weight, preferably sea bass,
  bonito *or* mackerel
1 teaspoon salt
4 tablespoons vegetable oil
1 tablespoon sweet soy sauce
1 teaspoon *sambal ulek*

Split fish down the backbone. Rub with salt.

Heat oil in a small saucepan and add 2 tablespoons water, soy sauce and *sambal ulek*. Stir frequently.

Roast fish over a charcoal fire and baste with this liquid mixture until fish is well done. Serve.

# Ikan Kari (Curried Fish)

1 whole fish, about 1½ lb (650 g) dressed
  weight, preferably porgy *or* sea bass
1 teaspoon salt
2 tablespoons vegetable oil
1 large onion, sliced
2 cloves garlic, chopped
2 teaspoons curry powder *or*
  1 teaspoon turmeric
  ½ teaspoon cummin
  ½ teaspoon coriander
  pinch of ginger
1 tablespoon coconut, desiccated or freshly
  grated
1 teaspoon *sambal ulek*
1 tablespoon tamarind juice

Rub fish all over with salt.

Sauté onion lightly in oil, subsequently adding chopped garlic and curry powder. Stir continuously to prevent the curry from burning.

Add coconut and *sambal ulek*. Fry for about 5 minutes and add 1 cup of water. Bring liquid to a boil.

Add fish. Cover and simmer 15 to 20 minutes. Finally, add tamarind juice just before serving.

# Sambal Goreng Ikan (Spiced Fish)

1 whole fish, about 1½ lb (650 g) dressed
   weight, preferably porgy *or* sea bass *or* carp
1½ teaspoons salt
½ cup flour
oil for deep-frying
1 large onion, sliced thinly
2 tablespoons vegetable oil
1 tablespoon *sambal ulek*
1 tablespoon tamarind juice

Rub fish with 1 teaspoonful of salt. Then cover it with flour, deep-fry and drain on absorbent paper, keeping fish warm.

Prepare sauce by lightly sautéeing sliced onion in oil, then adding *sambal ulek*, tamarind juice, ¼ cup water and salt. Bring the mixture to boil slowly, lower heat and simmer for 10 minutes.

Place fish in serving dish and pour sauce over it. Serve immediately.

*Alternative Method:* In this instance, use 1 fish of 1 lb (450 g) dressed weight, preferably porgy *or* sea bass *or* gurami. Cut into serving portions. Everything follows in the same manner, the difference being that this method is designed for steaks from larger fish, notably the cod, haddock or pollock.

# Ikan Teri Goreng (Fried Anchovy)

2 tablespoons vegetable oil
1 medium onion, sliced finely
1 teaspoon *sambal ulek*
1 lb (450 g) anchovy *or* smelt (fresh or frozen)
1½ teaspoons salt
½ cup coconut milk from ½ coconut
1 tablespoon tamarind juice

Heat oil in pan and sauté onion lightly. Add *sambal ulek* and stir.

Next, add fish and salt, stirring repeatedly so as to cover fish thoroughly with the spices.

Coconut milk and tamarind juice are then added. Cover the pan and simmer until liquid is absorbed by the fish. Serve warm.

# Ikan Goreng Asam Manis
# (Sweet and Sour Fish)

1 whole fish, about 1-2 lb (450-900 g),
   preferably porgy, sea bass, carp *or* gurami
1 teaspoon salt
1 egg
2 tablespoons flour
oil for deep-frying

### Sweet and Sour Sauce

2 teaspoons soy sauce
3 teaspoons cornstarch mixed with 4
   tablespoons water
1 tablespoon tomato ketchup
¼ cup vinegar
½ cup water
4 tablespoons sugar

Scale fish with dull knife, removing the insides. Wash well. Make two diagonal slashes on both sides. Rub fish with salt.

Mix egg with flour and rub over fish, both inside and out.

Heat oil and deep-fry till brown. Remove from oil and drain. Place on an oval platter and keep warm.

Bring all ingredients making up Sweet and Sour Sauce to a boil, stirring constantly, and pour over fish just before serving.

Garnish fish with shredded carrots or bits of pineapple. Tomatoes and capsicums may also be used for garnishing. They may be fried lightly before serving.

# Udang Goreng Asam Manis
# (Sweet and Sour Shrimps)

1 dozen shrimps, medium-sized
1 teaspoon salt
1 egg
2 tablespoons flour
oil for deep-frying

Shell, devein shrimps and rub with salt.

Mix egg with flour and dredge shrimps in the batter.

Bring oil to a boil and deep-fry.

Serve with Sweet and Sour Sauce (see preceding recipe).

# Begedel Ikan (Fish Croquettes)

1 lb (450 g) cod steak *or* fillet
2 slices white bread
2 egg yolks, with egg whites
    reserved for later use
1 small onion, chopped finely
1 tablespoon parsley
1 teaspoon salt
breadcrumbs for coating
oil for deep-frying

Poach fish in 2 cups of water and then flake off flesh in little bits.

Remove crust from bread and soften in 2 tablespoons of water. Gently pull bread apart into small pieces.

Mix fish with egg yolk, onion, parsley, pieces of bread and salt. Roll mixture into balls about the size of apricots or smaller.

Beat the egg whites until foamy. Dip balls in foamy egg whites first and then roll in breadcrumbs.

Deep-fry until medium brown and drain on paper towels. Serve.

*Note:* To make Shrimp or Crab Croquettes simply substitute with chopped raw shrimp or crab.

# Udang Kari (Shrimp Curry)

1 tablespoon vegetable oil
1 medium onion, chopped finely
2 cloves garlic, chopped finely
1 teaspoon turmeric
½ teaspoon cummin
1 teaspoon lemon grass
1 teaspoon *sambal ulek*
sliver of shrimp paste
1 teaspoon salt
1 cup coconut milk from ½ coconut
1 lb (450 g) shelled fresh or frozen shrimps

Heat oil and lightly sauté onion and garlic. Add turmeric, cummin and lemon grass. Stir and add *sambal ulek*, shrimp paste and salt. Stir again.

Add coconut milk and bring to a boil. Lower heat and add shrimps. Simmer uncovered for 15 to 20 minutes.

# Sambal Goreng Udang (Spiced Shrimps)

2 tablespoons vegetable oil
1 medium onion, chopped finely
2 cloves garlic, chopped finely
2 candlenuts, grated
1 teaspoon coriander
pinch of cummin
½ teaspoon turmeric
1 teaspoon *sambal ulek*
sliver of shrimp paste
1 lb (450 g) shelled fresh or frozen shrimps
½ teaspoon lemon grass
½ cup coconut milk from ½ coconut
2 *salam* leaves
1 teaspoon salt

Heat oil, then lightly sauté onion, garlic, grated candlenuts, coriander, cummin, turmeric, *sambal ulek* and shrimp paste.

Add shrimps and lemon grass. Fry lightly.

Now add coconut milk and bring to a slow boil. Lower heat, add *salam* leaves and salt. Simmer uncovered for about 15 and 20 minutes. Serve.

# Sambal Goreng Udang Kering (Spiced Dry Shrimps)

*illustrated on page 27*

1 lb (450 g) shrimps
1 teaspoon salt
2 tablespoons vegetable oil
2 cloves garlic, chopped finely
1 teaspoon *laos*
½ teaspoon lemon grass
sliver of shrimp paste
1 tablespoon coconut, desiccated or freshly
  grated
2 teaspoons *sambal ulek*

Leaving shrimps in their shells, sprinkle with salt and boil in water. Cool and peel the shrimps. Set aside.

Heat oil and sauté garlic, *laos* and lemon grass. Add shrimps, shrimp paste and coconut. Stir continuously and fry until coconut becomes lightly brown.

Add *sambal ulek* and fry for 5 minutes. Serve.

# Udang Pancet Saus Mentega (Butterfly Shrimps)

1 dozen large shrimps
1 small piece tamarind
3 cloves garlic, chopped
1 slice ginger
3 tablespoons sweet soy sauce
2 teaspoons cornstarch
3 tablespoons margarine

Cut shrimps lengthwise along the back, but do not remove shell. Remove black vein and wash well. Mix shrimps with all ingredients except margarine.

Heat margarine and fry shrimps for about 10 to 15 minutes.

# Udang Goreng Asam Garam Riau (Riau Salt and Sour Lobster)

2 medium lobster tails *or* any crayfish
2 tablespoons tamarind juice
1 teaspoon sweet soy sauce
½ teaspoon salt
2 tablespoons margarine *or* peanut oil

Scrub the shell, split it open from the underside, and get rid of the black vein. Slice into portions.

Mix tamarind juice, soy sauce and salt. Rub solution into lobster.

Heat oil in pan and fry lobster portions until light brown. Serve hot.

# Cumi-cumi Kalimantan (Borneo Squid)

½-1 lb (225-450 g) squid
1 tablespoon tamarind juice
2 tablespoons sweet soy sauce
1 teaspoon salt
2 tablespoons vegetable oil

Pull off the head of the squid and remove the ink sac. Clean the insides thoroughly. Cut into serving portions. Rub with tamarind juice, soy sauce and salt.

Heat oil in pan and add squid. Sauté until done, stirring continuously.

# Bebotok Kepiting Jawa
# (Javanese Chopped Crab)

*illustrated on page 28*

¼ roll shrimp paste
½ cup coconut milk from 1 coconut
1 medium onion, chopped finely
2 cloves garlic, chopped finely
2 candlenuts, grated
1 teaspoon coriander
pinch of cummin
pinch of turmeric
1 piece lemon grass
1 teaspoon *sambal ulek*
½ teaspoon salt
2 eggs, beaten slightly
1 lb (450 g) crab meat
1 lime leaf

Soften shrimp paste in coconut milk. Mix onion, garlic and candlenuts in a deep bowl, and then stir these 3 with the shrimp paste-coconut milk liquid.

Add coriander, cummin, turmeric, lemon grass, *sambal ulek* and salt. Add slightly beaten eggs and crab meat.

Fashion crab patties and place in aluminium foil, rolling foil so that it is both air-tight and water-tight.

Put patties in a double-boiler, cover and steam for about 1 hour. Add lime leaf. Serve warm.

*Note:* A novel serving suggestion is to cook the crab patties in the shells instead of using aluminium foil. Both pretty and convenient to handle!

# Sop Jagung Telur Kepiting
# (Corn and Crab Soup)

1 16-oz (450 g) can cream corn
2 cups water *or* clear chicken broth
2 teaspoons cornstarch mixed with some broth
1 teaspoon soy sauce
½ teaspoon sugar
1 cup cooked crab meat
1 egg white, beaten slightly

Mix all ingredients in a saucepan, except for crab meat and egg white. Stirring constantly bring mixture to a boil over medium heat.

Add crab meat, bring to a boil again, turn off heat and stir in egg white. Serve immediately.

*Note:* To add flavour to soup, serve with a separate dish of wine vinegar and one of soy sauce mixed with hot pepper. Each diner adds his own vinegar or soy sauce to taste.

# Poultry

The Asian's fondness for chicken and other dishes made from both domesticated fowl and game-birds rivals that of the average Westerner. However, while chicken has been reduced in the West to everyday or regular fare, replaced by turkey or beef on festive occasions, in Asia it remains the fowl of distinction, rivalled perhaps only by duck. Asian fondness for chicken is not of missile-age vintage. The voluminous court records of imperial China, as early as 1000 B.C., tell of farmers raising poultry for meat and eggs. Nor is this especially surprising. The fact is that today's popular domesticated chickens, the familiar supermarket variety, are Asian in origin — descendants of the red and green jungle-fowls.

The red jungle-fowls, whose wings are brilliant, cherry-red, roam the area from Bangladesh and southern China to Malaysia, Java and Sumatra. They are relatively common in scrub country and jungle clearings at low and reasonably moderate altitudes. The green jungle-fowl, a neighbouring cousin, inhabits Java and the insular stepping stones at the eastern tip of the island: Bali, Lombok (where the hottest chillies are grown), Sumbawa, Sumba, Flores and Timor. Bold creatures with bronzy red and green wings, they are often found near rice-fields. They also enjoy the rocky terrain along parts of the craggy coast.

America's internationally celebrated Plymouth Rocks and Rhode Island Reds, for example, share a common Javanese ancestry, as do all other domesticated chickens. In the early nineteenth century, in the heyday of the Yankee clipper, when the Sumatra spice run was on a commuter basis, returning skippers brought to New England — in addition to spices and recipes acquired in Asian ports — various types of red and green jungle-fowl, some wild, some domesticated. At this juncture the American farmer

took over. By careful selection and cross-breeding, the size, colour, shape and habits of these fowls underwent a radical transformation. Where meat was the objective, poultrymen chose fowls of large size that grew rapidly and cross-bred them until a suitable strain was found; where eggs were the objective, hen-breeding proceeded along similar lines.

It is easy to distinguish between wild and domesticated chickens in the market-place. The Asian jungle-fowls are thin, have small combs and hold their tails at disdainfully low angles compared to the domesticated types; jungle-fowls also often have feathered legs. In terms of meat quality, the wild birds are more stringy and tougher than their domesticated counterparts. For that matter, compared to Western chickens, Indonesian domesticated ones are also stringy and on the thin side. The American chicken is too plump, for example, its meat too sweet, sometimes so fulsome as to be tasteless and bland. Curiously, a tough, scrawny chicken is not only a challenge to the cook, but the bird is actually tastier than a plump chicken when prepared in the highly spiced Indonesian style. I sometimes suspect that the meat of stringy, gamy Asian birds is better able to absorb marinating and basting sauces than the pampered scientifically raised Western strains.

The best chickens for Indonesian recipes are fryers or broilers (as they are called in the US). These are tender, young, active birds, usually 10 to 16 weeks old. They have a small amount of fat and soft bones. In weight they average 1-3 pounds (450-1350 g). For the recipes here, use about 2½-pound (1125 g) chickens. Cooked in spices, sweet soy or coconut milk, they provide a welcome twist in cooking an old favourite. Indeed, Indonesians, as the rice table testifies, prefer many twists. In Indonesia, a chicken is often quartered and then cooked four different ways to add still more variety to the meal.

This emphasis on cooking chicken is somewhat misleading. In addition to chicken, Indonesia and neighbouring Asia abound in duck and game-birds such as jungle partridge, quail and pheasant. Incidentally, a tip to hunters: a game-bird may be substituted for chicken in these spicy Indonesian recipes. The result is a superb, unforgettable dish that borders on the sensational. I have eliminated them from these recipes since game-birds are not commercially available to the average housewife. Cornish hens are too small, although they are sometimes reminiscent of Indonesian chickens.

The ducks of Indonesia, by the way, are similar to those found on Long Island — fat and succulent. The islands are well stocked with mallard, teal and pintail. Here, as elsewhere in Asia, the Chinese must be credited with cooking them in the most delectable manner; Sino-Indonesian restaurants, in this regard, are perhaps unrivalled except for fabled Peking (but not having been there, I do not really know). In the highlands around Bandung, the mountain capital of western Java, turkeys are raised for the handful of foreigners in residence in Jakarta. However, in Southeast Asia the best turkeys are the frozen Australian birds readily available at Singapore supermarkets; when we lived in Indonesia, visiting foreign correspondents often brought turkeys as gifts. One American Thanksgiving Day there was a disaster. George Rice and the late Peter Gruening of United Press arrived with a bird. I rushed to our village *pasar* for some berries. I was horrified when I returned; Roemina, my kitchen helper, to be helpful, had diced the big bird in true Indonesian style! So much for visions of roast turkey in a tropical setting.

Before delving into the poultry dishes, a final note: in the preparation of Nasi Goreng or Indonesian fried rice, leftover chicken, duck and turkey may be used with abandon; indeed, leftovers are encouraged. In our household, within a week of a national holiday, such as Thanksgiving, my hungry household are whetting their appetites for Nasi Goreng *à la* turkey.

# Ayam O (Chicken O)

1 broiler or fryer, about 2½ lb (1125 g)
2 teaspoons salt
½ teaspoon ground black pepper
3 tablespoons vegetable oil *or* margarine
3 cloves garlic, chopped finely
pinch of ginger
1 teaspoon brown sugar
¼ roll shrimp paste, dissolved in 2 tablespoons
    water
2 scallions, both bulb and shoot, diced
2 tablespoons sweet soy sauce

Cut chicken into serving portions. Wash thoroughly. Rub thoroughly with salt and pepper and let chicken stand for about 10 minutes.

Heat oil in a pan, add chicken followed by garlic. Fry chicken and garlic until light brown.

Now add ginger and brown sugar and stir. Add dissolved shrimp paste and again stir well. Fry for about 2 minutes.

Mix in scallions and soy sauce, cover mixture, lower heat and cook for about 30 minutes. Add a little water if necessary to prevent drying. Serve.

# Ayam Kecap (Soy Chicken)

1 broiler or fryer
2 teaspoons salt
3 tablespoons vegetable oil
1 medium onion, chopped finely
pinch of nutmeg, grated
3 tablespoons sweet soy sauce
½ teaspoon tamarind juice

Cut chicken into servable portions and rub thoroughly with salt.

Heat oil in a large, heavy frying pan with a tight-fitting cover. Then add chicken and fry until light brown, stirring frequently to prevent it from sticking to the pan.

Combine onion with chicken and fry until onion turns mellow brown.

Then add nutmeg, soy sauce and tamarind juice, stirring well. Fry the mixture for about 20 minutes. Add 1 cup water, cover and simmer over low heat from 20 to 30 minutes. Serve.

# Ayam Besengek (Chicken Besengek)

1 broiler or fryer
2 teaspoons salt
3 tablespoons vegetable oil
2 medium onions, chopped finely
2 cloves garlic, chopped finely
2 red chillies, crushed
1 teaspoon ground coriander
pinch of ground cummin
1 teaspoon ground *laos*
2 candlenuts, grated
½ teaspoon shrimp paste
2 tablespoons coconut, desiccated or freshly
   grated
2 cups coconut milk from 1 coconut
1 teaspoon brown sugar
1 tablespoon tamarind juice

Cut chicken into serving portions and rub with salt. Fry in oil until light golden brown.

Add onion and garlic to chicken and fry until onion turns medium brown.

Now add chilli, coriander, cummin and *laos* and fry again for about 1 minute. Add candlenuts to mixture and stir well. Add shrimp paste and grated coconut. Fry an additional minute. Then add coconut milk and brown sugar. Simmer over low heat for about 30 minutes. Finally add in tamarind juice. Serve.

# Rempah Ayam (Spiced Chicken Cakes)

1 large chicken breast, about 1 lb (450 g)
1 slice white bread
1 clove garlic, chopped
1 small onion, chopped
¼ red chilli, crushed
1 teaspoon ground coriander
pinch of ground cummin
2 tablespoons coconut, desiccated or freshly
   grated
1 egg, beaten slightly
sliver of shrimp paste
1 teaspoon salt
breadcrumbs
3 tablespoons vegetable oil

Remove white meat from breast bone. Place meat on wooden board and chop finely.

Separately, remove crust from bread. Crumble bread into small pieces. Mix chicken and bread in a bowl.

Combine garlic and onion with chicken mixture. Then add crushed chilli, coriander, cummin, coconut, egg, shrimp paste and salt. Mix thoroughly.

Shape into small patties, sprinkle with breadcrumbs and fry on both sides in oil until medium brown. Serve.

# Ayam Kuning (Yellow Chicken)

1 broiler or fryer
½ teaspoon ground coriander
½ teaspoon *laos*
2 teaspoons salt
3 tablespoons vegetable oil
1½ teaspoons turmeric
1 medium onion, sliced thinly
2 cloves garlic, chopped
2 candlenuts, grated
pinch of lemon grass
2 cups coconut milk from 1 coconut
1 tablespoon tamarind juice

Cut chicken into serving portions. Rub thoroughly with a mixture of coriander, *laos* and salt.

Fry chicken in oil until medium brown. Add turmeric and fry an additional 2 minutes. Add onion and garlic and fry for a further 1 minute. Add candlenuts together with lemon grass and stir well. Finally add coconut milk and tamarind juice and simmer over low heat for about 30 to 45 minutes. Serve.

# Ayam Kari Jawa (Javanese Curried Chicken)

1 broiler or fryer
2 teaspoons salt
3 tablespoons vegetable oil
1 large onion, chopped
3 cloves garlic, chopped
1½ teaspoons turmeric
1 teaspoon coriander
½ teaspoon cummin
1 teaspoon *laos*
½ teaspoon lemon grass
1 red chilli, crushed
1 cup coconut milk from ½ coconut

Cut chicken into small portions and rub thoroughly with salt.

In a skillet fry chicken in vegetable oil until golden brown. Remove chicken and in the same skillet fry onion and garlic until medium brown. Add turmeric, coriander and cummin mixture. Fry for 1 minute, stirring continuously. Now add *laos*, lemon grass and chilli.

Return chicken to skillet and mix thoroughly with curry mixture. Add coconut milk and cook uncovered until chicken is tender. Serve.

Opor Ayam (p. 50)

Soto Ayam (p. 52)

Ikan Bali (p. 32)

Ayam Panggang Sumatra (recipe on opposite page)

# Ayam Panggang Sumatra
# (Sumatran Barbecue Chicken)

*illustrated on page 48*

1 small broiler or fryer
2 tablespoons sweet soy sauce
2 tablespoons tamarind juice
3 tablespoons margarine
1 teaspoon salt
3 red chillies, crushed

Cut chicken into 4 parts and parboil for 10 minutes.

In a saucepan, heat soy sauce, tamarind juice, margarine and salt over low heat. Remove as soon as margarine melts. Next add crushed chillies to mixture and mix well.

Marinate chicken in spicy mixture for 15 minutes.

Broil over red-hot, smokeless charcoal fire, basting frequently with mixture. Serve hot from fire.

# Ayam Pekalongan (Pekalongan Chicken)

*A favourite dish in central Java. It derives its name from Pekalongan, a sleepy, dusty, Javanese town near the southern coast of the island.*

1 broiler or fryer
2 tablespoons vegetable oil
1 large onion, chopped finely
2 cloves garlic, chopped finely
1 teaspoon *laos*
1 red chilli, crushed
¼ roll shrimp paste
2 teaspoons salt
3 tablespoons tamarind juice
½ cup coconut milk from ½ coconut

Place chicken in a large saucepan. Make sure that the chicken is covered with sufficient water, and let it simmer until tender. Remove chicken from stock, cool and debone. Dice chicken.

Separately, in a heavy skillet, heat oil and fry onion and garlic until light brown. Add *laos* and crushed chilli and stir well. Then add chicken with shrimp paste and salt.

Fry chicken until almost dry, stirring frequently. Now add tamarind juice and coconut milk. Cover and cook until stock is almost completely absorbed by chicken. Serve.

# Ayam Smor (Braised Chicken)

1 fryer, about 3 lb (1¼ kg)
2 teaspoons salt
3 tablespoons vegetable oil
1 large onion, sliced
2 cloves garlic, chopped
pinch of chopped ginger
pinch of nutmeg
1 teaspoon ground coriander
½ teaspoon ground black pepper
sliver of shrimp paste
1 teaspoon soy sauce
1 tablespoon tamarind juice

Cut chicken into serving portions and rub with salt. Fry pieces in vegetable oil until light brown.

Add onion and garlic, frying until onion turns light brown. Now add ginger, nutmeg, coriander, black pepper, shrimp paste and soy sauce. Fry ingredients for about 1 minute.

Add 1 cup water and tamarind juice. Cover tightly. Simmer over low heat until chicken is tender. Serve.

# Opor Ayam (Chicken in Coconut)

illustrated on page 45

1 broiler or fryer
2 teaspoons salt
1 large onion, chopped finely
3 cloves garlic, chopped finely
3 tablespoons vegetable oil
1 tablespoon coriander
pinch of chopped ginger
1 teaspoon ground lemon grass
2 cups coconut milk from 1 coconut
1 *salam* leaf

Cut chicken into serving portions and rub with salt.

Fry onion and garlic in vegetable oil until light brown. Now add coriander, ginger and lemon grass. Stir well and fry for about 1 minute.

Add chicken, mixing thoroughly so that chicken absorbs the spices. Add coconut milk and *salam* leaf. Cover tightly and cook over medium heat for about 40 minutes. Serve.

# Ayam Abon-abon (Shredded Chicken)

1 large chicken breast, about 1 lb (450 g)
½ teaspoon ground coriander
½ teaspoon ground *laos*
2 tablespoons tamarind juice
1 teaspoon salt
2 tablespoons vegetable oil

Place chicken breast in saucepan and cook for 20 minutes until tender. Remove from stock. Cool and shred meat from breast bone.

Place chicken in bowl and add coriander, *laos*, tamarind juice and salt. Mix thoroughly.

Now fry chicken in vegetable oil in a heavy skillet, stirring frequently until meat is dry and crisp. Serve as a *rijsttafel* garnish.

# Ayam Goreng Rempah (Spicy Fried Chicken)

1 fryer, about 3 lb (1¼ kg)
2 cloves garlic, chopped finely
1 teaspoon ground black pepper
1 teaspoon lemon grass
1 teaspoon coriander
sliver of shrimp paste
1 teaspoon soy sauce
1 tablespoon tamarind juice
2 teaspoons salt
3 tablespoons vegetable oil

Cut chicken into small pieces and marinate in mixture of garlic, pepper, lemon grass, coriander, shrimp paste, soy sauce, tamarind juice and salt. Leave for at least 30 minutes.

Heat oil in a heavy skillet, then fry the chicken uncovered until deep golden brown. Stir constantly so that the chicken does not stick to the pan. If necessary, a small amount of water may be used for this purpose. Serve immediately.

# Soto Ayam (Spicy Chicken Stew)

*illustrated on page 46*

1 small broiler or fryer
3 teaspoons salt
vegetable oil for frying
1 large onion, sliced thinly
1 tablespoon margarine
2 cloves garlic, chopped
5 peppercorns
pinch of turmeric
pinch of chopped ginger
4 oz (120 g) thin egg noodles or mung bean
  noodles
1 finely chopped scallion, reserving both bulb
  and shoot
1 cup bean sprouts, washed and cleaned

Cut chicken into small portions and place in heavy skillet with 4 cups water and salt. Cover and cook over low heat until chicken is tender. Remove chicken from stock but reserve the stock for later use. Let chicken cool, then debone and fry in oil until brown. Set aside.

Separately fry onion in margarine until deep brown. Remove from skillet and put aside.

In the same skillet fry garlic, peppercorns, turmeric and ginger for about 2 minutes. Pour this mixture into chicken stock.

Cook noodles in boiling chicken stock.

Add scallion to stock, simmering over low heat for about 10 minutes.

Place some bean sprouts and chicken into soup bowls and then add the soup mixture. Sprinkle with fried onion and serve.

# Ayam Bumbu Rujak
# (Chicken in Pungent Sauce)

1 broiler or fryer
1 large onion, chopped finely
2 cloves garlic, chopped finely
3 tablespoons vegetable oil
1 teaspoon brown sugar
1 red chilli, crushed
2 candlenuts, grated
¼ roll shrimp paste
1 tablespoon tamarind juice
1 teaspoon sweet soy sauce
2 teaspoons salt

Cut chicken into serving portions.

Fry onion and garlic in oil until golden brown. Add brown sugar, chilli, candlenuts and shrimp paste and stir. Add chicken to this spicy mixture.

Then add tamarind juice, soy sauce, 1 cup water and salt. Cover tightly and cook slowly until liquid is completely absorbed by chicken. Serve.

# Ayam Bawang (Chicken with Onions)

1 fryer, about 3 lb (1¼ kg)
3 teaspoons salt
½ teaspoon ground black pepper
3 tablespoons margarine *or* vegetable oil
3 cloves garlic, crushed
pinch of chopped ginger
1 teaspoon *laos*
½ red chilli, crushed
2 tablespoons tamarind juice
1 tablespoon sweet soy sauce
10 small white onions, peeled

Cut chicken into serving portions. Rub thoroughly with salt and black pepper. Now fry chicken parts in margarine or oil until medium brown.

Add crushed garlic, ginger and *laos*. Stir-fry for about 1 minute. Then add crushed chilli, tamarind juice and soy sauce. While stirring, add 1 cup water and whole onions. Cover and simmer over low heat for about 30 minutes. Serve.

# Ayam Makassar (Macassar Chicken)

2 chicken breasts, about 1 lb (450 g) each
1½ teaspoons coriander
pinch of cummin
½ teaspoon ground black pepper
3 tablespoons coconut, desiccated or freshly
  grated
3 tablespoons vegetable oil
1 cup coconut milk from ¼ coconut
1 teaspoon lemon grass
3 lime leaves
1 teaspoon salt

Remove chicken meat from breast bone and chop into fine pieces.

Separately, sauté coriander, cummin, black pepper and grated coconut in vegetable oil until coconut starts to brown.

Now add chicken meat to mixture and stir well. After this add coconut milk, lemon grass, lime leaves and salt. Cook uncovered until almost dry, stirring occasionally. Serve.

# Ayam Ternate (Ternate Chicken)

*Although this dish is popular on fabulous Ternate it conspicuously omits the spice that made Ternate famous and drew rival Dutch, Portuguese and Spanish merchants in the sixteenth century — nutmeg. For a short time, Ternate rivalled Banda as the world's primary source of nutmeg and mace (the outer covering of the nutmeg).*

**1 broiler or fryer**
**pinch of ginger**
**1 teaspoon lemon grass**
**3 candlenuts, grated**
**2 teaspoons salt**
**3 tablespoons vegetable oil**
**1 large onion, sliced**
**3 cloves garlic, chopped**
**1 red chilli, crushed**
**sliver of shrimp paste**
**2 tablespoons tamarind juice**
**3 lime leaves**
**1 cup coconut milk from ½ coconut**

Cut chicken into small pieces.

Mix together ginger, lemon grass, candlenuts and salt. Rub chicken with this spicy mixture.

Fry chicken in oil until golden brown. Now add onion and garlic until onion turns light brown. Combine with chilli, shrimp paste, tamarind juice and lime leaves. Fry an additional minute, stirring constantly.

Add coconut milk and cook uncovered over low heat until liquid is almost completely evaporated or absorbed. Serve.

# Bebek Panggang (Barbecue Duck)

**1 duckling, about 3 lb (1¼ kg)**
**2 teaspoons salt**

**Barbecue Sauce**

**3 tablespoons sweet soy sauce**
**2 tablespoons tamarind juice**
**½ or more red chilli, crushed**
**2 tablespoons vegetable oil**

Quarter duckling. Place in a heavy saucepan and add 1 teaspoon salt and 1 cup water. Cook over low heat for about 20 minutes. Remove duckling from stock.

Separately, combine soy sauce, tamarind juice, chilli, oil and 1 teaspoon salt.

Baste duckling with this sauce and place quartered pieces on grill over red-hot, smokeless charcoal. Baste frequently. Cook until duckling is crisp and brown. Serve.

# Bebek Smor (Braised Duck)

1 duckling, about 3 lb (1¼ kg)
3 teaspoons salt
2 medium onions, chopped finely
2 cloves garlic, chopped finely
2 tablespoons vegetable oil
1 teaspoon coriander
2 candlenuts, grated
2 *salam* leaves
sliver of shrimp paste
juice and rind of ½ lemon

Cut duckling into serving portions. Place in large saucepan. Add salt and 3 cups water and cook over low heat until tender. Remove duckling pieces from stock.

Fry onion and garlic in oil until mellow brown. Add coriander and candlenuts and mix thoroughly.

Finally, add duckling together with *salam* leaves, shrimp paste, lemon juice and rind. Cook, covered, over very low heat until liquid is almost entirely absorbed. Serve.

# Bebek Smor Kecap (Braised Soy Duck)

1 duckling
2 tablespoons honey *or* brown sugar
½ cup soy sauce
1 piece star anise *or* 1 cinnamon stick
1 slice ginger
3 cloves garlic

Place all the ingredients in a large pot. Cook over medium heat until duckling is tender. Cut into serving portions and place on an oval dish. Place the remaining gravy in a separate dish. Serve.

*Note:* If powdered ginger is used, do use it sparingly.

# Burung Darah Goreng (Fried Pigeon)

2 pigeons
2 tablespoons honey
3 tablespoons soy sauce
2 cloves garlic, crushed
½ teaspoon salt
oil for deep-frying

Wash pigeons well, rub inside and outside with mixture of honey, soy sauce, garlic and salt.

Bring oil to a boil and deep-fry pigeons until brown.

Cut into small pieces and serve, while still hot, on a bed of lettuce.

To make a perfect dip, mix equal amounts of salt and freshly ground pepper.

*Note:* This dish may be made equally well with chicken.

# Meat

In Indonesia, the cooking of beef has evolved into a fine art. A hallmark of Indonesian beef dishes is the art of marinating. No festive rice table is complete without beef, and it usually appears in several forms — shredded, dried, steamed or curried. But for the most part, Indonesian beef is stringy, tough and gamy. Choice cuts are different from those in the West, and frequently there is little choice of cuts. Beef, moreover, is expensive in the islands and is therefore used sparingly. It is prepared with as little waste as possible.

The main sources of domesticated cattle are the slate-coloured water-buffalo, a sluggish draught animal which delights in wallowing in water and mud, and the ubiquitous hump-backed white Brahmin steer which does double duty hauling a bullock cart. Since these animals are comparable to tractors, they represent a heavy capital investment and are social status symbols on par with the Mercedes-Benz-cum-mink syndrome in the West, and are apt to avoid an early trip to the slaughter house. But since herds of buffalo crossing roads and highways are common sights, the casualty rate is reasonably high — and so is the number of unexpected feasts in villages, contiguous to the main traffic arteries.

The most popular methods used in the preparation of beef in Indonesia are sautéeing, braising, fricasseeing and frying with aromatic, pungent and searing spices, particularly cinnamon, nutmeg, coriander and crushed red chilli. In Indonesia, sautéeing involves the browning of slivers of meat and spices in a heavy skillet lightly greased with margarine, coconut or peanut oil. In braising and fricasseeing, slivers or cubes of meat which have already been sautéed are cooked in a covered saucepan or stewed in a thick liquid together with vegetables and additional spices. In Indonesian frying, as in the West, the cooking of the meat is done in an inch or two of margarine or vegetable oil.

Argentine, American or Australian beef by itself is superb: they are the 'Three A's' of the beef world. Prepared in the Indonesian style the beef acquires added lustre. Any fine-grained, firm and lean, American beef is suitable for the rice table; my own preferences are for either boneless, top sirloin or top round. I use minute steaks in the preparation of *satay* or skewered meat.

Beef, of course, is not the only meat consumed with gusto in Indonesia. Goat is also popular as are lamb and mutton. Here again 'Three A's' lamb and mutton are of superior quality and ideally suited in the dishes that follow.

In one respect, however, Indonesia presents a somewhat startling picture on the meat sector. Indonesia, with the exception of Malaysia, is probably the only Moslem country in the world where large quantities of pork are consumed. The Indonesian Moslems, who constitute about ninety per cent of the population, will not, of course, touch pork (quite literally). But on Hindu Bali, in the Christian areas of Sumatra, Sulawesi, Maluku and the Lesser Sundas, and among the Sino-European-influenced communities in the bigger cities, pork is widely sold. The islands themselves abound in wild swine. These tusked beasts are as dangerous as they are brave, and often raid padi fields close to villages. They are also meat eaters and have been known to take on a python. Pig hunts are common in West Java and south-east Sumatra, where the swine hide in forests of teak and in the swampy jungle interior (Indonesian swine are good swimmers; likewise Indonesian tigers).

On Bali, pig-raising is commercially profitable and pigs going to market in bamboo baskets are daily sights – their destinations: Singapore, and Chinese shops in Kalimantan and peninsular Malaysia. The Balinese pig, I can testify, is among the world's finest. On one of our trips to Bali, a close group of friends from Ubud presented us at the airfield with a surprise departure gift – a *babi berguling* or suckling pig roasted over a spit and basted, Balinese style, with a spicy marinade. From Bali we flew home to Java with visions of a sumptuous feast in the making.

As you will quickly observe in the next few pages, the beef and pork recipes are strongly suggestive of Chinese influence, particularly in the fine slicing or dicing of the meat. There is also a distinct Indian or Pakistani touch in the curried dishes, although it should be stressed that Indonesian curry is unlike the curry found on the subcontinent. The addition of Indonesian spices and techniques have transported these Sino-Indian-style dishes to new heights.

# DENDENG

*Dendeng* is a popular style of meat preservation in Indonesia. The meat is invariably sliced thinly, rubbed with spices, herbs and salt and set out to dry in the sun. It can be kept almost indefinitely. Indonesians prepare *dendeng,* in order of popularity, from venison, buffalo, beef, and beef liver. This mode of preservation may be characterized as spicy, dry refrigeration. It probably was extremely popular in medieval Europe and the need for spices motivated the later voyages of discovery. Obviously, the method has no place in the modern kitchen. But it remains a superb type of food even when freshly prepared.

*Dendeng* is simple to prepare, and a must.

# Dendeng Manis (Sweet Dried Beef)

1 lb (450 g) round beef
1 teaspoon coriander
pinch of cummin
1 teaspoon *laos*
½ teaspoon nutmeg
1 tablespoon brown sugar
1 teaspoon salt
2 tablespoons vegetable oil
1 onion, chopped
1 clove garlic, chopped
sliver of shrimp paste
1 teaspoon tamarind juice

Slice beef into thin strips. Marinate meat with a mixture of coriander, cummin, *laos,* nutmeg, brown sugar and salt.

Heat oil in a pan and add meat, frying until medium brown. Add onion and garlic and fry for about 1 minute. Then add shrimp paste, tamarind juice and 1½ cups water, cover and simmer until completely dry. Serve.

# Dendeng Santan (Coconut Dried Beef)

*illustrated on page 67*

1 lb (450 g) round beef
2 cloves garlic, chopped finely
2 candlenuts, grated
½ teaspoon coriander
1 tablespoon tamarind juice
1 teaspoon brown sugar
1 teaspoon *laos*
1 teaspoon salt
2 tablespoons vegetable oil
½ roll shrimp paste
½ cup coconut milk from ½ coconut

Cut beef into slender slices. Rub meat first with garlic and candlenuts followed by coriander, tamarind juice, brown sugar, *laos* and salt.

Separately, dissolve shrimp paste in a little coconut milk.

Now heat oil in a pan and fry meat until it turns a medium brown. Then add shrimp paste. Cover and cook until almost dry.

The final touch: add coconut milk and stir well. Cover and cook again until dry.

# Begedel Cabe (Peppered Beef Croquettes)

½ lb (225 g) ground beef
2 egg yolks, reserving egg whites
1 clove garlic, chopped finely
1 scallion, chopped finely
1 tablespoon parsley, chopped
1 teaspoon lemon grass
pinch of ginger
1 teaspoon coriander
1 teaspoon salt
12 red chillies
breadcrumbs
vegetable oil for deep-frying

Knead beef with egg yolk and then with garlic and scallion. Add, one at a time, parsley, lemon grass, ginger, coriander and salt. Set aside.

Slit chillies lengthwise, remove seeds and stuff with beef. Then beat egg whites until foamy and coat the top of beef. Sprinkle with breadcrumbs and deep-fry. Drain on absorbent paper towels. Serve.

# Rendang Padang (Padang Beef)

1 tablespoon vegetable oil
2 cloves garlic, chopped finely
1 teaspoon turmeric
½ teaspoon ginger
3 lemon grass leaves
1 lb (450 g) top round or lean beef, sliced thinly
2 or more red chillies, crushed
1 teaspoon or more salt
1½ cups coconut milk from 1 coconut
1 salam leaf

Heat oil in pan and add garlic, turmeric, ginger and lemon grass. Sauté lightly.

Then add meat and crushed chillies. Sauté 3 minutes, stirring frequently. Add salt and chillies and mix well.

Pour coconut milk over meat and add salam leaf. Cover and cook over low heat until almost dry. Serve.

# Gulai Koja (Dried Curried Beef)

1 lb (450 g) boneless round beef
1 teaspoon tamarind juice
1 teaspoon salt
2 tablespoons vegetable oil
1 clove garlic, chopped
5 small onions, sliced thinly
1 teaspoon rice flour
½ teaspoon turmeric
pinch of cloves
pinch of cummin
pinch of ginger
1 teaspoon coriander
2 pieces mace
1 cinnamon stick
1½ cups coconut milk from 1 coconut

Cut beef into thin slices and rub thoroughly with tamarind juice and salt.

Heat oil. Sauté meat and garlic lightly. Now add onions and sauté until golden brown.

Separately, mix rice flour with turmeric, cloves, cummin, ginger and coriander. Pour mixture over meat and mix well. Fry for about 1 minute and then add mace, cinnamon stick and coconut milk.

Cover and cook over low heat until meat is almost dry. Serve.

# Daging Abon-abon (Shredded Spicy Beef)

1 lb (450 g) boneless chuck
2 cloves garlic, chopped
1 teaspoon brown sugar
1 teaspoon *laos*
½ teaspoon coriander
1 tablespoon tamarind juice
1 teaspoon salt
2 tablespoons vegetable oil
1 small onion, sliced thinly

On the day before, cook meat in water with a bit of salt until tender. Store overnight in refrigerator. The following day shred beef into small strips, pulling it apart with your fingers.

Mix together garlic, brown sugar, *laos*, coriander, tamarind juice and salt. Add mixture to meat and stir well.

Heat oil in heavy skillet and fry meat-cum-spices until deep brown and crisp.

Separately, fry onion until deep brown. Sprinkle on top of meat and serve.

# Empal Daging (Diced Spicy Beef)

1 lb (450 g) stewing beef
1½ teaspoons salt
1 teaspoon *laos*
1 tablespoon tamarind juice
3 tablespoons vegetable oil

Dice beef in the Irish-stew fashion and cook with salt and 2 cups water until tender. Allow to cool in bouillon, and then remove.

Rub beef with *laos* and tamarind juice. Heat oil in pan and fry beef until medium brown. Serve.

# Daging Smor (Braised Beef)

1 lb (450 g) boneless chuck
2 tablespoons oil
2 medium onions, sliced into thin strips
½ teaspoon nutmeg
2 tablespoons sweet soy sauce
1½ teaspoons salt

Cut beef into broad slices.

Heat oil and fry onions until light brown. Remove onions and fry beef in the same pan until golden brown. Now add nutmeg and soy sauce. Stir briskly. Add fried onions, salt and 2 cups water. Cover and simmer until meat is tender. Serve.

# Begedel Pedes
# (Spicy Beef Croquettes)

½ lb (225 g) ground beef
1 medium potato
1 egg yolk, reserving egg white
1 teaspoon ground black pepper
pinch of nutmeg
½ teaspoon salt
1 medium onion, chopped
breadcrumbs
3 tablespoons vegetable oil

Boil, then mash potato. Mix beef and mashed potato. Knead egg yolk into beef mixture. Add pepper, nutmeg and salt, mixing thoroughly. Add onion to mixture. Shape into patties.

Beat egg white until foamy and coat patties. Dip patties into breadcrumbs and sauté in oil on both sides until brown. Serve.

# Sapi Kari Palembang
# (Palembang Curried Beef)

illustrated on page 66

2 tablespoons vegetable oil
1 medium onion, sliced
2 cloves garlic, chopped
2 or more red chillies, crushed
pinch of cloves
pinch of cummin
pinch of ginger
1 teaspoon turmeric
1 lb (450 g) stewing beef
1½ teaspoons salt
2 cups coconut milk from 1 coconut
1 *salam* leaf
1 large potato, boiled and diced

Heat oil in pan and sauté onion, garlic, chillies, cloves, cummin, ginger and turmeric. Do not burn the mixture.

Dice beef and add to spices together with salt. Sauté until spices are absorbed by beef, stirring frequently. Add coconut milk and *salam* leaf. Cover and simmer until almost tender.

About 20 minutes before removing from heat, add potato. Serve warm.

# Bebotok Sapi (Indonesian Meat Loaf)

illustrated on page 65

½ lb (225 g) ground beef
1 small onion, chopped finely
2 cloves garlic, chopped finely
2 candlenuts, grated
1 teaspoon coriander
pinch of cummin
pinch of ginger
½ or more red chillies, crushed
pinch of lemon grass
1 tablespoon tamarind juice
½ teaspoon salt
2 tablespoons vegetable oil
1 cup coconut milk from ½ coconut
1 egg, hard-boiled and sliced thinly

Combine beef with onion and garlic. Add candlenuts and then coriander, cummin, ginger, chillies, lemon grass, tamarind juice and salt. Mix well.

Heat oil in a pan and fry beef and spices until medium brown. Add coconut milk. Simmer until almost dry.

Cut out 7 in x 7 in (18 cm x 18 cm) aluminium foil squares. On each square, place a slice of egg and then cover with a heaped tablespoonful of beef mixture. Wrap meat in foil and seal ends.

Steam in a double boiler for about 1 hour. Serve.

*Note:* As a variation, substitute either shrimp, veal, chicken or fish (cod is excellent) for beef. In Indonesia, *bebotok* is wrapped in banana leaves. If you prefer a natural substitute, however, use cabbage leaves instead of foil. The result is a form of Indonesian stuffed cabbage.

# Sambal Goreng Daging (Peppered Beef)

1 lb (450 g) round steak or any tender cut
1 medium onion, chopped finely
2 cloves garlic, chopped finely
2 tablespoons vegetable oil
1 teaspoon *laos*
1 teaspoon salt
¼ roll shrimp paste
½ teaspoon brown sugar
2 red chillies, sliced thinly
2 lime leaves
2 *salam* leaves
1 tablespoon tamarind juice
water *or* coconut milk (optional)

Slice beef thinly.

Sauté onion and garlic lightly in vegetable oil. Add *laos,* salt, shrimp paste and brown sugar. Fry for several minutes. Now mix beef with spices.

Add chilli, mix well and then add lime leaves, *salam* leaves and tamarind juice. Fry until deep brown. A little water or coconut milk may be added to prevent drying out and burning. Serve warm.

*Note:* Sambal Goreng Daging, which is common fare the length and breadth of the archipelago, may be made with liver.

# Sambal Goreng Hati (Spicy Beef Liver)

1 lb (450 g) beef liver
2 tablespoons vegetable oil
1 cup coconut milk from ½ coconut

### Spicy ingredients

1 large onion, chopped
3 cloves garlic, chopped
1 or more red chillies, crushed
1 teaspoon *laos*
½ teaspoon lemon grass
pinch of brown sugar
2 candlenuts, grated
3 lime leaves
sliver of shrimp paste
1 tablespoon tamarind juice
1 teaspoon salt

Boil liver in water with a pinch of salt for about 15 minutes. Remove from stock. Slice.

Combine the spicy ingredients. Sauté in oil for about 2 minutes.

Add liver, and sauté for an additional 2 minutes. Add coconut milk, cover and simmer until almost dry. Serve.

*Note:* Chicken liver may be used as a substitute, but it should not be boiled first.

# Rempah-rempah (Spicy Meat Cakes)

½ lb (225 g) ground beef
1 medium onion, chopped finely
1 clove garlic, chopped finely
½ cup coconut, desiccated or freshly grated
sliver of shrimp paste
½ teaspoon black pepper
½ teaspoon coriander
pinch of brown sugar
½ teaspoon salt
1 egg
vegetable oil for deep-frying

Knead beef with onion and garlic. Then thoroughly mix with coconut, shrimp paste, pepper, coriander, brown sugar and salt. Add an egg and mix well. Shape into tiny meatballs.

Deep-fry until medium brown. Drain on absorbent paper towels and serve.

# Lelawar Babi (Shredded Spicy Pork)

1 lb (450 g) boneless pork
1 small onion, chopped finely
2 cloves garlic, chopped finely
½ teaspoon cummin
1 teaspoon coriander
1 teaspoon *laos*
1 teaspoon salt
1 tablespoon vegetable oil
1 red chilli, diced
1 *salam* leaf
1 cup coconut milk from ½ coconut
1 tablespoon tamarind juice

Cut pork into thin strips. Mix onion and garlic with pork. Now rub pork with cummin, coriander, *laos* and salt.

Heat vegetable oil in a pan and add strips of pork. Sauté several minutes.

Add chilli, *salam* leaf and coconut milk, simmer uncovered until meat is very tender. Now add tamarind juice. Serve.

*Note:* Lelawar is a Balinese style of cooking and that is why pork is used. Beef may be substituted.

Bebotok Sapi (p. 62)

Sapi Kari Palembang (p. 62)

Dendeng Santan (p. 58)

Babi Tulang Cin (see opposite page)

# Babi Tulang Cin (Borneo Spare Ribs)

·illustrated on page 68

2 lb (900 g) meaty spare ribs
3 cloves garlic, chopped finely
2 tablespoons peanut oil
½ teaspoon nutmeg
pinch of cloves
½ teaspoon black pepper
2 teaspoons salt
1 teaspoon brown sugar
1 tablespoon soy sauce

Chop spare ribs into desired serving portions.

Fry garlic in oil until brown. Add spare ribs to pan and mix thoroughly with garlic. Then add nutmeg, cloves, pepper and salt. Sauté until the mixture turns a medium brown.

Now add brown sugar, soy sauce and ½ cup water. Cover tightly and simmer until tender.

# Babi Cin (Sino-Indonesian Pork)

2 small potatoes
2 tablespoons peanut oil
1 medium onion, sliced thinly
3 cloves garlic, sliced thinly
1 teaspoon coriander
pinch of cummin
½ teaspoon black pepper
½ teaspoon brown sugar
1 tablespoon soy sauce
1 teaspoon salt
1 lb (450 g) boneless lean pork

Boil potatoes in their jackets. When cool, peel and slice thinly. Set aside.

Heat up oil in a pan and sauté onion, garlic, coriander, cummin and pepper until light brown. Add brown sugar, soy sauce and salt. Combine pork with the mixture and fry over low heat for about 10 minutes, stirring frequently.

Add 1½ cups water, cover and simmer until tender.

Add sliced potatoes to the cooked pork. Serve.

# Babi Masak Kecap (Pork in Soy Sauce)

1 lb (450 g) lean boneless pork, diced
1 tablespoon peanut oil
2 small onions, chopped finely
3 cloves garlic, chopped finely
pinch of ground ginger
1 teaspoon brown sugar
3 tablespoons sweet soy sauce
1 teaspoon salt

Fry pork in peanut oil until light brown. Add onion and garlic. Stirring constantly, fry until onions turn brown.

Add ginger, brown sugar, soy sauce, ½ cup water and salt. Cover tightly and simmer 15 to 20 minutes. Serve.

# Babi Bali (Balinese Pork)

1 medium onion, chopped finely
3 cloves garlic, chopped finely
1 tablespoon peanut oil
1 or more red chillies
1 teaspoon coriander
1 teaspoon turmeric
1 lb (450 g) lean pork
1 cup coconut milk from 1 coconut
1 teaspoon salt

Sauté onion and garlic in oil together with chillies, coriander and turmeric for about 2 minutes.

Add pork and sauté an additional 5 minutes.

Now add coconut milk and salt. Cover and simmer over low heat until pork is tender. Serve.

# Sambal Goreng Babi (Spicy Pork)

1 lb (450 g) lean boneless pork, diced
1 tablespoon peanut oil
1 medium onion, chopped
2 cloves garlic, chopped
pinch of ginger
1 or more red chillies, crushed
1 teaspoon sweet soy sauce
1 teaspoon salt
2 chopped scallions, reserving both
  bulb and shoot

Fry pork in peanut oil until light brown. Add chopped onion and garlic, stirring frequently until onion is light brown.

Add ginger, chilli and soy sauce. Mix thoroughly. Then add salt and 1 cup of water. Cover and simmer for about 20 minutes.

Add scallions and cook over low heat for about 3 minutes. Serve.

# Babi Berguling
# (Spit-roasted Pig, Bali Style)

1 suckling pig, about 10 lb (4½ kg)
1 large onion, chopped finely
2 cloves garlic, chopped finely
3 whole cloves
1 teaspoon ginger
1 teaspoon coriander
½ red chilli, crushed
2 *salam* leaves
4 teaspoons turmeric
3 tablespoons salt
1 cup coconut milk from 1 coconut
2 tablespoons coconut, desiccated or freshly
  grated

Wash pig thoroughly in cool water in preparation for stuffing.

Mix together onion, garlic, cloves, ginger, coriander, chilli and *salam* leaves. Now add 2 teaspoons turmeric and 1½ tablespoons salt.

Stuff pig, rubbing interior thoroughly. Sew cavity.

Separately mix together remainder of turmeric and salt and rub into pig's skin.

Skewer pig and roast over red-hot smokeless charcoal fire. Rotate constantly. Brush pig occasionally with coconut milk mixed with desiccated coconut. Cook for approximately 4 hours until meat is tender and skin crisp.

# Satay

Until suburban living burst on the post-war American scene, it was reasonably accurate to observe that the cooking of skewered, diced meat over fiery coals was largely the imprint of Islamic influence on the world's cooking. In a broad scimitar-shaped area, extending from West Africa to Indonesia, skewered meat is one of the lively culinary arts. In Marakeesh and Casablanca, in Beirut and Damascus, Karachi and Dacca, Ipoh and Singapore, and along the island-chain of Indonesia, roasting bits of meat over a charcoal brazier is deeply embedded in the culture. Moving east of Suez, the marinating and basting sauces for this form of cookery becomes increasingly aromatic, pungent and searing in direct ratio to the abundance and variety of available herbs and spices. The artistic apogee in the preparation of skewered meats is in Indonesia, in the very 'Spice Islands' themselves.

Every country in the Islamic belt lays claim to having originated the art of skewering. Indeed there are as many claimants as names for this particular style of cooking. The Turks call it *sheesh-kebab* — *sheesh* meaning skewer, *kebab* meaning meat. In the Caucasian mountains, along the southern perimeter of Russia, where Islamic influence spread centuries ago, following the trail of spice-laden caravans, it is called *shashlik*. On the Indian subcontinent the term is romanized as *kabab*. In Southeast Asia, among the Malays and Indonesians, skewering is known as *satay* or *saté*.

The Chinese scoff at the theory that *satay* is Islamic in origin, although it is likely that it entered China through the backdoor, Xinjiang (Sinkiang). The Chinese not only claim to having originated the art but also contend that the words *satay* and *saté* are Chinese derivatives.

According to their version, early migrants from fabled Cathay, pre-dating the arrival of Arab traders and the advent of Islam, filtered southward into the region now called Southeast Asia. They brought with them the custom of roasting or grilling bits of pork, pierced on bamboo sticks, over red-hot charcoals. Invariably, for convenience as much as habit, the Chinese slipped three pieces of meat — never more, never less — onto the bamboo skewer. *Satay*, say the Chinese, therefore comes from the south Chinese words *sah* (three) and *tay* (piece). Gradually, the Malays and Indonesians copied the technique and, conceded the Chinese, crowned it with the decisive embellishment: spicy marination and a unique peanut sauce. With the adoption of Islam, which proscribes the pig, the Malay peoples substituted lamb, beef, fowl and seafood for pork.

Today the street hawker's cry of *satay* is as common in Indonesia as the chirp of the cricket in the evening. Barefoot pedlars in sarongs carrying a portable, charcoal stove, patter through coastal ports, inland towns and villages calling out their wares for all to hear. They are the masters of the trade and their *satay* is unrivalled. Often, while my husband covered cabinet sessions in Jakarta which lasted into dawn, we would squat with Indonesian newsmen outside the Premier's office at Pejambon, swapping *kabar angin* (literally, 'news on the wind'), while munching freshly grilled *satay kambing* made from marinated slivers of goat.

Personally, I have always found pork, chicken, lamb and goat the most succulent meats for *satay*. Quite unabashedly, I have always been glad that Moslems may not eat pork — that leaves that much more for the rest of us! However, on the Hindu island of Bali and among the Christian enclaves on Ambon, the Malukus, in Sulawesi and Sumatra, pork *satay* is, unfortunately, a prized dish. No festive occasion is complete without a touch of pork.

In contemporary America, with the emphasis on outdoor living and cooking, *satay, saté, shashlik, kebab,* skewered meat — call it what you will — has made a deep and probably lasting inroad into eating habits. But tragically, skewering in America is often the victim of the 'bigger and better' philosophy. The pieces of meat used are invariably far too large, the cooking coals aflame instead of inwardly afire, and skewers are sometimes laden like garbage scows with pineapples, tomatoes, etc., all at the expense of the meat. Harsh judgement? Perhaps. But though it makes the unskilful laugh, it cannot but make the artist grieve.

To skewer *satay* skilfully and successfully in the Indonesian fashion, six factors should be constantly borne in mind: (1) the charcoal, (2) the skewer, (3) the size and quality of the cuts, (4) rotation, (5) the preparation of the marinating and basting mixtures and (6) the preparation of the peanut sauce.

In order, then: first, the charcoals. What applies here applies to all outdoor cooking. In the impatient West, barbecues are often hastily prepared. The cook lights the charcoal (eventually), fans the air briskly and while the flames leap higher, starts to grill the meat. The end result, euphonically termed 'charcoal broiled', is often so burnt and blackened beyond recognition as to cause courteous guests to adopt a grin-and-bear-it posture. A cardinal rule in outdoor cooking is to fan the burning charcoals until the coals glow evenly without the presence of a flame. Think of the Indian fakir and his bed of live coals the next time you barbecue.

Next, the skewer. It should be as slender as the proverbial reed and tapered towards the tip like a fly-rod. Bamboo sticks, inexpensive and easily obtainable in Japanese gift and food shops in the West, are ideal and may be used repeatedly if you wrap the holding ends in aluminium foil before thrusting onto the red-hot coals. Metal skewers are as good, but avoid those with rapier points. In *satay,* the meat is not removed from the skewer before eating but is eaten straight from the stick. Too sharp a metal object is dangerous. Since *satay* is eaten from the skewer, the size of the portions should be relatively small, only slightly larger than a radish. This not only makes the meat easier to pull from the skewer, but facilitates the marination. Tender meat is advisable; top quality meat is recommended. The use of a commercial tenderizer is useful; in Indonesia (as in Surinam), the wrapping of meat in papaya leaves does the tenderizing trick. In the preparation of chicken *satay,* use only the breast.

During the skewering keep an eye on the meat, rotating from time to time to ensure even cooking and no burning. In the preparation of *satay,* the marinating sauce, used also for the basting process, is a key to ultimate success. Similarly, the *saus kacang* or peanut sauce, without which *satay* is like rolls without butter, must be carefully prepared.

Indonesian *satay* accompanied by peanut sauce is an incomparable outdoor dish. Learn the knack of making it and you will be serving it often through the summer season. It is delightful with a glass of beer. With rice and just one Indonesian-styled vegetable, *satay* constitutes a meal worthy of praise. Served as a snack, *satay* is an ideal cocktail titbit. A word of caution, however: there is never enough to go around.

# Satay Ayam (Chicken Satay)

2 chicken breasts
3 tablespoons vegetable oil
2 tablespoons sweet soy sauce
1 tablespoon tamarind juice
½ teaspoon coriander

Cut chicken into bite-size portions. Thread on bamboo sticks or metal skewers. Set aside.

Heating oil in saucepan, add the rest of the ingredients.

Using a soft-tufted cake brush, paint chicken thoroughly.

Place sticks in circular fashion over red-hot charcoals. Rotate skewers often and baste frequently to prevent chicken from drying out. Serve immediately.

# Satay Ayam Madura (Madura Chicken Satay)

2 chicken breasts
3 tablespoons vegetable oil
1 small onion, chopped finely
1 clove garlic, chopped finely
2 candlenuts, grated
2 tablespoons coconut, desiccated or freshly grated
1 teaspoon coriander
1 teaspoon *sambal ulek*
½ teaspoon lemon grass
⅓ roll shrimp paste, softened in 2 tablespoons water
1 teaspoon brown sugar

Cube chicken into portions and set aside.

Heat oil in saucepan and add the rest of the ingredients. Stir well.

Marinate chicken cubes in this mixture for at least 1 hour to allow the aromatic and pungent spices to be absorbed.

Skewer the meat and cook until well done over charcoal. Serve.

# Satay Ayam Kuning
# (Yellow Chicken Satay)

2 chicken breasts
3 tablespoons vegetable oil
½ teaspoon coriander
pinch of cummin
1 teaspoon turmeric
½ teaspoon salt
1 tablespoon tamarind juice

Cut chicken into bite-size portions. Thread on bamboo sticks or meat skewers. Set aside.

Heat oil in saucepan and add coriander, cummin, turmeric, salt and tamarind juice.

Using a soft-tufted cake brush, paint chicken thoroughly with the mixture.

Cook meat over charcoal till well done.

# Satay Kambing (Mutton Satay)

1 lb (450 g) boneless mutton
2 tablespoons vegetable oil
1 teaspoon shrimp paste, softened in 2
　tablespoons water
1 tablespoon dark soy sauce
1 teaspoon brown sugar
1 small onion ⎤
2 cloves garlic ⎦ chopped together

Cut mutton into bite-size portions and set aside.

Mix vegetable oil with the other ingredients.

Marinate meat for at least 2 hours.

Thread meat on skewers and broil over charcoal. Serve.

# Satay Babi Kuning (Yellow Pork Satay)

1 lb (450 g) boneless lean pork
1 small onion, chopped finely
1 clove garlic, chopped finely
1 candlenut, grated
½ teaspoon *laos*
½ teaspoon coriander
1 teaspoon turmeric
½ cup coconut milk from ½ coconut
1 tablespoon vegetable oil
1 teaspoon salt

Cut pork into thin slices.

Mix together all the rest of the ingredients.

Marinate pork for at least 2 hours.

Thread on skewers and broil over charcoal. Serve.

# Satay Udang sama Hati
# (Shrimp and Liver Satay)

1 lb (450 g) fresh shrimps
½ lb (225 g) beef liver
2 tablespoons margarine
1 clove garlic, chopped
1 tablespoon dark soy sauce
1 tablespoon tamarind juice
1 teaspoon salt

Boil shrimps for 15 minutes. Then remove shell and devein.

Separately, boil liver in 1 cup water for about 15 minutes. Cut cooked liver into small pieces.

Skewer shrimp and liver in alternating fashion, first shrimp, then liver, then shrimp and so on. Set aside.

Melt margarine in saucepan, and add in the rest of the ingredients. Brush shrimp-liver combination thoroughly with this mixture.

Broil quickly over red-hot coals and serve.

# Satay Babi (Pork Satay)

1 lb (450 g) boneless lean pork
1 clove garlic
2 candlenuts, grated
1 teaspoon shrimp paste, softened in 2
    tablespoons water
2 tablespoons dark soy sauce
2 tablespoons peanut oil

Cut pork into thin slices.

Mix together garlic, candlenuts, shrimp paste, soy sauce and peanut oil.

Marinate pork for two hours, permitting meat to soak up the sauce.

Thread pork on skewers and broil over charcoal. Serve.

*Note:* Pork requires slightly more time to broil than chicken or beef.

# Satay Sapi (Beef Satay)

1 lb (450 g) boneless sirloin or any tender cut
2 tablespoons vegetable oil
1 tablespoon sweet soy sauce
1 tablespoon tamarind juice

Cut beef into bite-size portions.

Heat oil and mix with soy sauce and tamarind juice.

Marinate beef in sauce for 15 minutes and then thread on skewers.

Broil over charcoal till done. Serve.

# Satay Sapi Manis (Sweet Beef Satay)

1 lb (450 g) boneless sirloin
2 tablespoons vegetable oil
1 teaspoon brown sugar
2 tablespoons sweet soy sauce
½ teaspoon salt

Cut meat into small portions.

Heat oil and add brown sugar, soy sauce and salt.

Marinate meat in sauce for 15 minutes and then thread on skewers.

Broil quickly over charcoal. Serve.

# Satay Sapi Pedes (Hot Beef Satay)

1 lb (450 g) boneless sirloin
1 small onion, chopped finely
3 tablespoons vegetable oil
1 teaspoon *sambal ulek*
2 candlenuts, grated
1 teaspoon coriander
pinch of ginger
2 tablespoons tamarind juice

Cut meat into small portions.

In a saucepan, sauté onion in oil until medium brown. Remove pan from fire and set aside.

Meanwhile mix together all the other ingredients. Add the resulting mixture to the sautéed onions.

Marinate beef in this mixture for 15 minutes.

Thread skewers and broil quickly over charcoal. Serve.

# Satay Tusuk Anak Sapi (Veal Satay)

1 lb (450 g) boneless veal
1 small onion, chopped finely
1 tablespoon vegetable oil
½ teaspoon turmeric
pinch of lemon grass
1 teaspoon coriander
1 teaspoon salt
1 teaspoon brown sugar
½ roll shrimp paste
1 tablespoon tamarind juice
1 cup coconut milk from ½ coconut

Cut veal into small portions.

Sauté onion lightly in oil in a saucepan. Add turmeric, lemon grass and coriander. Stir and sauté again.

Add meat to pan with salt and brown sugar. Sauté lightly.

Then add shrimp paste, tamarind juice and coconut milk. Cover saucepan and cook until almost dry.

Remove meat and thread on skewers.

Hold skewers over red-hot coals for only a few minutes and serve immediately.

# Saus Kacang Tidak Pedes (Bland Peanut Sauce)

4 tablespoons smooth peanut butter
1 clove garlic, chopped finely
sliver of shrimp paste
1 teaspoon brown sugar
1 tablespoon dark soy sauce
1 tablespoon tamarind juice
1 teaspoon salt

Mix peanut butter and ¾ cup water in a saucepan and bring to a boil. Turn off heat and stir to a paste consistency.

Add the rest of the listed ingredients and stir well. Serve lukewarm with satay.

# Saus Kacang Baru (Fresh Peanut Sauce)

1 small onion, sliced thinly
2 cloves garlic, sliced thinly
1 tablespoon peanut oil
1 cup peanuts, roasted and shelled
1 piece lemon grass
1 piece *kencur*
1 tablespoon shrimp paste
1 red chilli, crushed
1 teaspoon brown sugar
1 tablespoon dark soy sauce
½ teaspoon salt
2 tablespoons tamarind juice

Fry onion and garlic in oil until brown.

Run onion, garlic, peanuts, lemon grass, *kencur* and shrimp paste through a grinder or blender.

To this blended mixture add chilli, brown sugar, soy sauce, salt and tamarind juice. Mix together thoroughly.

Now add enough boiling water to make a thick paste. Serve with satay.

# Saus Kacang Pedes (Hot Peanut Sauce)

1 medium onion, sliced finely
1 clove garlic, sliced finely
1 tablespoon margarine
3 tablespoons smooth peanut butter
2 teaspoons *sambal ulek*
1 teaspoon brown sugar
1 tablespoon sweet soy sauce
1 tablespoon tamarind juice
sliver of shrimp paste
½ teaspoon salt

Sauté onion and garlic in margarine until deep brown. Remove from pan and drain on paper towel.

Add peanut butter and ½ cup water to saucepan and bring to a boil. Turn off heat and stir to a paste consistency.

Add *sambal ulek*, brown sugar, soy sauce, tamarind juice, shrimp paste and salt, and mix well.

Now add onion and garlic and stir gently. Serve lukewarm or cool.

*Note:* For a different variation, leave out onion.

# Sambal Kecap (Spicy Soy Sauce)

4 tablespoons dark soy sauce
1 red chilli, sliced
1 teaspoon tamarind juice
1 tablespoon fried onions

These ingredients, when mixed together, serve as an excellent satay dip.

# Vegetables

Vegetables in the Spice Islands are familiar to Westerners; indeed, some are of New World origin. With some scattered exceptions making the rule, an Indonesian, buying vegetables in a European or American market, would feel completely at home — glass, chromium, stainless steel and fluorescent lights notwithstanding.

Climate, of course, is the factor controlling the cultivation of all plant life, including vegetables. And climate depends largely on altitude. Although the Malay world is situated along the equator, it rises from below sea-level to snow-capped peaks. Java, Sumatra and Sulawesi are studded with a jumble of active and extinct volcanoes and escarpments. Rivers rush down the mountain slopes and deposit volcanic silt into valleys and onto lowlands. The result is an enriched soil.

Although Java is crowded to bursting point, with a population of upwards of ninety million people, the island still has pockets of rain-forests and bamboo groves. At different elevations the heat and humidity of the island subtly changes. So does the island's produce.

From sea-level to 305 metres, rice and rubber flourish; at 1,525 metres, strawberries; above 1,525 metres, tea, coffee and orchids, and at extreme altitudes, rhododendrons, maple and a wide variety of 'Western' vegetables. In a real sense, Indonesia is the world's largest greenhouse, shaped like a pyramid and with controlled temperature and humidity at ascending levels.

Curiously, in Indonesia the temperate and torrid zones share the same latitude. In Irian Jaya (Western New Guinea), the pinnacle is reached, with snow-trimmed mountains. Thus, in Indonesia it is possible to cultivate a wide variety of completely unrelated vegetables, from bamboo shoots and breadfruit to cauliflower and cabbage. Indonesian cookery has exploited this natural advantage. The result is very often a familiar 'Western' vegetable in a strange setting.

Some Indonesian vegetables, of course, are exotic, such as the flower of the papaya tree. Others are relatively common and reflect a large measure of Chinese cooking influence in the islands: snow peas (young peas in pod) and bean sprouts. But, for the most part, Indonesians use familiar vegetables. Among them are *bayem, terung* and *ketimun* (spinach, eggplant and cucumber). And there are *kacang kaprie* and *kacang panjang* (peas and yard-long beans). Other Indonesian favourites have Dutch names, which indicate that they may be European in origin and most probably were introduced during the Dutch colonial period which goes back to the sixteenth century. These include *kol* or *kool* (cabbage), *buncis* (string bean), *wortel* (carrot) and *tomat* (tomato).

Indonesians delight in one vegetable which Europeans do not generally eat but which is immensely popular in the Americas, North, Central and South. This is *jagung* or corn. Indeed, on the island of Madura, off the north-eastern coast of Java, corn is the staple, not rice. The Madurese roast their corn over hot coals, or, like most of the islanders, fashion them into small cakes.

Peas are also extremely popular the length and breadth of Indonesia. They are not served as a dish by themselves, however; rather, a handful of peas is scattered into different vegetable dishes, almost at random. In their cooking of vegetables, the Indonesians also make greater use of mustard greens (*sawi*) and leeks (*prei*) more than any other people.

In the vegetable recipes which follow, I have eliminated the picturesque but hard-to-procure vegetables and concentrated on the use of familiar vegetables. Many of these vegetable dishes are ideally suited for a Western buffet.

Two points should be made in advance: the recipes using *sambal ulek* or its substitute, Italian-style crushed red pepper, are fiery and dry. The mild-tasting vegetables are usually not only mild but also wet. Indeed, Sayur Lodeh, a common vegetable dish in Indonesia, takes the form of a soup, although it is not served as a soup course. You merely pour the vegetables and their broth over your rice and add side-dishes. In some of the following recipes, such as Cap Cai Ca, Chinese influence is manifest.

Some of the Indonesian vegetable dishes call for the use of shrimp. At first glance, it would appear that these recipes have been misplaced in this volume and belong under the Fish and other Seafood heading. But these dishes are essentially vegetable dishes. To bring out the flavour of certain vegetables, the Indonesians have ingeniously developed the technique of using shrimp. I have never found this method employed anywhere outside of Southeast Asia and nowhere to such an extent as in the archipelago.

# Sambal Goreng Tempe (Fermented Soybeans)

3 compressed soybean cakes, sliced thinly
oil for deep-frying
1 onion, sliced thinly
4 cloves garlic, chopped
3 red chillies, sliced thinly
1 teaspoon *laos*
1 teaspoon brown sugar
1 tablespoon tamarind juice
½ cup dried shrimp, soaked in water for about 30 minutes

Deep-fry sliced soybean cakes in hot oil. Drain and set aside.

In separate pan, fry onion, garlic and chillies in 1 tablespoon of oil. Add *laos*, brown sugar and tamarind juice.

Mix in fried soybean cakes and soaked shrimp. Fry for several minutes. Serve.

*Note:* If you happen to be in a lazy mood, here is a short cut. Fry soybean cakes. Drain. Mix with 1 tablespoon readymade *sambal ulek*, or any available prepared *sambal*. Presto — Sambal Goreng Tempe.

# Sambal Goreng Terung (Peppery Eggplant)

*illustrated on page 85*

2 small eggplants
1 tablespoon tamarind juice
½ teaspoon salt
1 small onion, sliced thinly
2 tablespoons vegetable oil
1 teaspoon coriander
½ teaspoon brown sugar
1 or more red chillies, crushed
⅓ roll shrimp paste softened in 1 tablespoon water

Peel eggplants and slice thinly; if a firmer texture is preferred, leave skin and slice. Sprinkle with tamarind juice and salt.

Sauté onion lightly in oil and add coriander, brown sugar and chillies. To the same pan add shrimp paste, and stir well.

Add eggplant and mix thoroughly with onion and spices. Sauté in uncovered pan for about 10 minutes. A little water may be added to prevent burning. Serve warm.

*Note:* Never cover pan, otherwise eggplant will soften and turn into a paste consistency.

# Sambal Goreng Buncis
# (Peppered String Beans)

1 lb (450 g) string beans
1 medium onion, sliced thinly
1 tablespoon vegetable oil
1 red chilli, crushed
1 teaspoon lemon grass
1 teaspoon *laos*
½ teaspoon brown sugar
pinch of cloves
1 teaspoon salt
1 teaspoon shrimp paste softened in 2
   tablespoons water
½ cup coconut milk from ½ coconut

Remove strings from beans and slice each bean into 3 segments.

Sauté onion lightly in oil together with chilli, lemon grass, *laos*, brown sugar, cloves and salt.

Then add shrimp paste and string beans. Mix thoroughly. Sauté about 3 minutes.

Add coconut milk, cover tightly and cook over low heat until string beans are tender. Serve warm.

# Sambal Goreng Hati sama Buncis
# (Spicy String Beans with Chicken Livers)

1 lb (450 g) string beans
3 chicken livers, sliced into slivers
1 tablespoon vegetable oil
1 small onion, chopped finely
½ teaspoon turmeric
pinch of ground cloves
½ teaspoon lemon grass
1 teaspoon brown sugar
1 red chilli, crushed
1 teaspoon salt
¼ cup coconut milk from ⅓ coconut
⅓ roll shrimp paste softened in 2 tablespoons
   water

Remove strings from beans and slice each bean in half.

Sauté chicken livers in oil with onion, stirring frequently. Add turmeric, cloves, lemon grass, brown sugar, chilli and salt. Sauté for 2 minutes.

Add string beans followed by coconut milk. Mix thoroughly and add shrimp paste. Cover and cook over low heat until tender.

*Note:* This dish improves in flavour if left overnight in the refrigerator and then reheated before serving.

# Sambal Goreng Kool (Hot Cabbage Sauté)

1 medium onion, sliced finely
1 tablespoon vegetable oil
1 or more red chillies, crushed
sliver of shrimp paste
1 teaspoon brown sugar
1 teaspoon *laos*
1 teaspoon salt
1 medium cabbage, cut coarsely

Sauté onion lightly in oil. Add chilli, shrimp paste, brown sugar, *laos* and salt. Sauté for about 1 minute, mixing frequently.

Add cabbage, stir and cover. Cook over low heat until cabbage wilts. If necessary, add a small amount of water or coconut milk to prevent burning. Serve warm.

# Sambal Goreng Prei (Peppered Leeks)

1 lb (450 g) leeks
1 tablespoon vegetable oil
1 or more red chillies, crushed
½ teaspoon brown sugar
1 teaspoon salt
1 tablespoon tamarind juice
¼ cup coconut milk from ½ coconut

Slice leeks into 1-in (2½-cm) pieces.

Heat oil in pan. Add chillies and brown sugar. Mix thoroughly.

Add leeks and salt. Stir, then add tamarind juice and coconut milk.

Cover pan and cook until leeks are tender. Serve warm.

# Sambal Goreng Tomat (Peppered Tomatoes)

*illustrated on page 85*

1 tablespoon vegetable oil
1 small onion, sliced finely
1 clove garlic, chopped finely
1 or more red chillies, crushed
1 teaspoon *laos*
½ teaspoon salt
4 firm tomatoes, preferably partially ripe
1 teaspoon brown sugar
½ teaspoon salt
¼ cup coconut milk from ⅓ coconut

Heat oil in pan and add onion, garlic, chillies, *laos* and salt. Sauté lightly.

Quarter tomatoes and, together with brown sugar and salt, add to the same pan. Mix thoroughly.

Then add coconut milk, cover and cook tomatoes to porridge consistency. Serve.

Sambal Goreng Terung (p. 82) and Sambal Goreng Tomat (see opposite page)

Begedel Jagung (p. 92)

Gado-gado (p. 93)

Sambal Goreng Telur (p. 97) and Sambal Goreng Tahu (see opposite page)

# Sambal Goreng Bloemkool
# (Peppered Cauliflower)

1 medium cauliflower
1 tablespoon vegetable oil
1 small onion, sliced thinly
1 teaspoon *laos*
1 or more red chillies, crushed
sliver of shrimp paste
½ teaspoon brown sugar
1 teaspoon salt
1 cup coconut milk from 1 coconut

Pull cauliflower apart to make florets.

Heat oil in pan and sauté onion lightly. Add cauliflower florets and sauté an additional 2 to 3 minutes.

Add *laos,* chillies, shrimp paste, brown sugar and salt. Sauté another minute.

Add coconut milk and cover tightly. Lower heat and cook until florets are tender. Serve.

# Sambal Goreng Tahu
# (Peppered Bean Cakes)

*illustrated on page 88*

3 bean cakes
2 tablespoons vegetable oil
1 small onion, chopped
pinch of ginger
2 cloves garlic, chopped finely
1 scallion, chopped finely
1 red chilli, chopped finely
1 celery stalk, chopped finely
½ teaspoon salt
1 tablespoon dark soy sauce

Slice bean cakes into thin pieces. Sauté bean cake until light brown and remove from pan.

In same pan, add onion and ginger. Sauté until light brown. Then add bean cake, garlic, scallion, chilli, celery and salt. Sauté until almost tender.

Add soy sauce. Serve.

# Sambal Goreng Lombok (Lombok Peppers Sauté)

1 dozen green chillies
2 tablespoons vegetable oil
1 small onion, chopped finely
2 cloves garlic, chopped finely
1 teaspoon brown sugar
½ teaspoon shrimp paste
1 tablespoon tamarind juice
½ teaspoon salt
¼ cup coconut milk from ⅓ coconut

Cut chillies lengthwise, remove seeds and slice thinly.

Heat oil in pan and sauté onion and garlic lightly together with brown sugar, shrimp paste, tamarind juice and salt.

Now add chillies and sauté until wilted.

Finally, add coconut milk and cook uncovered until almost dry. Serve.

# Sayur Lodeh (Vegetables and Shrimp)

*(See cover photograph)*

*Although this common vegetable dish takes the form of a soup, it is not served as a soup course. The vegetables and their broth are poured over the rice and side-dishes are added.*

1 tablespoon vegetable oil
1 medium onion, sliced finely
1 clove garlic, sliced finely
1 teaspoon coriander
1 teaspoon *laos*
½ lb (225 g) shelled fresh or frozen shrimps, cut into thin slices
1 red chilli, crushed
½ lb (225 g) cabbage, chopped coarsely
½ lb (225 g) cauliflower, parted into florets
1 small carrot, diced
½ lb (225 g) string beans, removing strings and cut into 3 parts each
1 small eggplant, cubed
1½ teaspoons salt
3 cups coconut milk from 1 coconut
1 *salam* leaf

Heat oil in pan and sauté onion lightly. Add garlic, coriander and *laos*. Fry for 1 minute.

Add shrimp and sauté for 2 minutes.

Add chilli, cabbage, cauliflower, carrot, string beans, eggplant and salt. Cover and cook over low heat for about 10 minutes.

Then add coconut milk and *salam* leaf and cook uncovered, stirring almost continuously, until vegetables are tender. Serve.

*Note:* Chicken can be substituted for shrimps, chicken breast being preferable.

# Sayur Bayem (Indonesian-style Spinach)

1 lb (450 g) spinach
1 small onion, sliced finely
1 clove garlic, chopped
2 cups coconut milk from ½ coconut
sliver of shrimp paste
salt to taste

Wash spinach thoroughly and set aside. Place onion and garlic in a saucepan with coconut milk, shrimp paste and salt. Bring to a boil.

Add spinach to the pan. Cook uncovered until tender. Serve.

# Sayur Kari (Curried Vegetables)

1 tablespoon vegetable oil
1 teaspoon turmeric
½ teaspoon cummin
½ teaspoon *laos*
½ teaspoon coriander
1 carrot, cubed
2 medium potatoes, peeled and diced
2 cups coconut milk from 1 coconut
salt to taste
1 small eggplant, peeled and diced
½ lb (225 g) string beans, removing strings
   and cut into 3 parts each
½ lb (225 g) cabbage, chopped coarsely

Heat oil in pan and add turmeric, cummin, *laos* and coriander. Sauté lightly.

Add carrots and potatoes with 1 cup coconut milk. Add salt to taste. Cover and cook for about 10 minutes.

Add eggplant, beans, cabbage and remaining coconut milk. Cover and continue cooking until carrots and potatoes are tender. Serve.

# Sayur Kool (Indonesian Cabbage)

1 tablespoon vegetable oil
1 small onion, chopped finely
1 clove garlic, chopped finely
1 medium cabbage, cut coarsely
2 cups coconut milk from ½ coconut
sliver of shrimp paste
1 red chilli, crushed
1½ teaspoons salt
½ lb (225 g) shelled fresh or frozen shrimps
1 tablespoon tamarind juice

Heat oil in pan and add onions and garlic. Fry lightly. Add cabbage and sauté until wilted.

Then add coconut milk, shrimp paste, chilli and salt. Bring to a boil.

Add shrimp and cook uncovered for about 10 minutes, stirring constantly.

Finally add tamarind juice and serve.

# Begedel Jagung (Corn Croquettes)

*illustrated on page 86*

3 ears young corn
1 whole scallion, chopped finely
½ teaspoon *laos*
½ teaspoon coriander
pinch of black pepper
2 tablespoons flour
2 eggs
pinch of salt
3 tablespoons margarine

Remove kernels from cob, slicing downward in swift strokes with paring knife.

Mix together all other ingredients except margarine to prepare a batter.

Melt margarine in pan and pour batter into it by the tablespoon, forming round cakes.

Fry on both sides till done, and then serve. Makes about 8 delicious cakes.

*Note:* It may also be deep-fried in a large amount of boiling oil.

# Sayur Asam (Sour Vegetables)

1 lb (450 g) string beans, with strings
   removed and each cut into 3 parts
1 small onion, chopped finely
1 clove garlic, chopped finely
2 tablespoons tamarind juice
sliver of shrimp paste
1 teaspoon *laos*
1½ teaspoons salt
1 lb (450 g) shelled fresh or frozen shrimps

Place everything, except the shrimps, in a saucepan. Stir, cover and cook over low heat until beans are tender.

Now add shrimps and bring to a boil. Lower heat and cook uncovered for 10 minutes. Serve.

*Note:* A handful of shelled raw peanuts is good for flavouring.

# Pare-pare (Stuffed Bitter Gourd)

2 medium bitter gourds
½ lb (225 g) ground pork
1 onion, chopped
2 cloves garlic, chopped
3 tablespoons light soy sauce
2 tablespoons vegetable oil

Cut one end of each bitter gourd off and remove seeds. Parboil gourd for about 10 to 15 minutes.

Mix ground pork with all the rest of the ingredients except oil, and stuff lightly into bitter gourds.

Heat oil and fry stuffed bitter gourd on both sides until light brown. Add 1 cup of water, cover tightly and cook for about 30 to 40 minutes over medium heat.

# Gado-gado (Indonesian Salad)

*illustrated on page 87*

1 bean cake
1 teaspoon vegetable oil
1 small cabbage, chopped coarsely and boiled
½ lb (225 g) string beans, removing strings, halved and boiled
½ lb (225 g) spinach, parboiled
1 bunch watercress, parboiled
½ lb (225 g) fresh bean sprouts, scalded
1 small cucumber, peeled and sliced
2 eggs, hard-boiled, shelled and cut into quarters
shrimp wafer, crumbled

Sauté bean cake in vegetable oil until brown. When cool slice into bite-size portions.

In each dish place desired amount of cabbage, beans, spinach, watercress and bean sprouts. Garnish with cucumber, eggs, bean cake and crumbled shrimp wafer.

Serve Gado-gado with peanut sauce (see next recipe), either poured over the dish or, if preferred, separately.

# Gado-gado Saus Kacang (Gado-gado Peanut Sauce)

1 tablespoon oil
1 onion, chopped
1 clove garlic, chopped
4 tablespoons smooth or coarse peanut butter
3 green chillies, crushed
pinch of lemon grass
1 teaspoon brown sugar
sliver of shrimp paste
1 tablespoon tamarind juice
1 teaspoon sweet soy sauce
1 teaspoon salt
½ cup coconut milk from ¼ coconut

Heat oil and fry onion and garlic. Set aside.

Mix peanut butter with ½ cup water and bring to a boil. Remove from heat and add chillies, lemon grass, brown sugar, shrimp paste, tamarind juice, soy sauce and salt.

Add in onion and garlic and mix thoroughly.

Stir in coconut milk and when the mixture is smooth, simmer over low heat. Serve atop Gado-gado or separately in a gravy boat.

*Note:* If a spicy-hot sauce is preferred, simply increase the amount of chillies.

# Sawi Asin (Salted Mustard Greens)

mustard greens
salt
rice water

Wash mustard greens thoroughly. Take a generous amount of salt and bruise the stalks, making sure that salt reaches all parts. Make small bundles and tie with strings. Place in crock or glass jar.

Before boiling rice for the next meal, wash the rice in a large amount of water. Pour over the vegetables and be sure the vegetables are completely immersed.

The pickled greens should be ready in 4 or 5 days; they go well mixed with cooked pork.

# Cap Cai Ca
# (Mixed Vegetables, Sino-Indonesian Style)

1 lean pork chop
1 teaspoon salt
1 chicken breast
pinch of ginger
2 tablespoons peanut oil
1 medium onion, chopped
2 cloves garlic, chopped
½ lb (225 g) shelled fresh or frozen shrimps
1 tablespoon soy sauce
1 small cabbage, chopped coarsely
2 leeks, chopped coarsely
2 teaspoons cornstarch dissolved in 3
   tablespoons water

Dice pork, removing bone. Place pork in saucepan, add ½ cup water and ½ teaspoon salt. Cover and bring to a boil.

Place chicken in a separate saucepan, adding 1 cup water, ½ teaspoon salt and ginger. Cook until tender. Remove chicken and dice. Save chicken bouillon.

In a larger pan heat oil, add onion and garlic and sauté lightly. Then add pork, chicken, shrimp and soy sauce. Mix thoroughly.

Add chicken bouillon. Bring to a boil. Add cabbage and leeks to boiling mixture and cook for only a few minutes so that vegetables retain crispness.

Finally add cornstarch mixture and bring to a boil. Remove and serve.

With white rice and some crushed red peppers, this dish constitutes a meal in itself.

# Eggs

It is said of the egg that perhaps no other single article of food can be used in so many intriguing ways. This is certainly borne out by the wide usage of eggs in both Occidental and Oriental cooking. In contemporary Asia, as in the West, the egg is considered a rich source of nutrition. Little wonder; nine eggs, the equivalent of a pound in weight, has the nutritive value of one pound of beef. Thus in impoverished lands the egg is often a substitute for meat, although the poverty of some areas is so deep that people prefer to raise fowls to eggs, and sell rather than consume their poultry and its by-product.

In Indonesia, on the main islands of Java, Sumatra and Sulawesi, and along the tiny bracelet of islands embracing Bali and known as the Nusa Tenggara chain, domesticated fowl is plentiful, and, therefore, so are eggs. Every village maintains its own flock of chickens, ducks or geese; the last do double-duty as sentries at night, creating an awful din should anyone approach the village. However, if you are from a Western background and are accustomed to chicken eggs, it would be wise in Indonesia to specify chicken eggs (*telur ayam*) in a restaurant or hotel. Otherwise, the likelihood is that you will be served a slightly rubbery egg with a hard, yellow yolk and bluish colouring — a duck egg.

Indonesians prize the duck egg with cause.

Although the Javanese are often portrayed as abstruse, they also have an earth-bound, practical side. Indonesians simply prefer the duck egg because it is larger than the chicken egg and you can therefore get more nourishment from it. Nobody can argue with such realism. But having been accustomed to chicken eggs, I find that it requires stoic discipline and the reorientation of prejudices to sit down to a plate of duck eggs. Baking, of course, is another story. In the United States, duck eggs are the favourite of the commercial baker and for the same reason that the Indonesian farmer is impressed. This disingenuity is not confined solely to the Western world; the Chinese are also rather cool to duck eggs and most Chinese restaurants hide them in their superb soups. But the diner is unaware of this, and nobody can argue with Chinese soup — the world's finest — particularly the fabulous melon and asparagus and crab-egg soups of Glodok, Jakarta's Chinese quarter.

The following Indonesian egg recipes invariably call for the duck egg. But except for the first recipe (*telur asin*), chicken eggs are recommended, white or brown, and preferably in the smaller-graded size.

# Telur Asin (Salted Eggs)

10 duck eggs
1 lb (450 g) coarse salt
½ teaspoon saltpetre

Place the eggs in an old-fashioned earthen jar or bean pot.

Dissolve salt and saltpetre in 8 cups boiling water. Leave to cool.

Pour over eggs and store for 3 weeks.

When required, remove eggs from bean pot and hard-boil them. Serve, each sliced in half, but retaining the shell.

# Dadar Jawa (Omelette Java)

5 eggs
1 whole scallion, chopped finely
sliver of shrimp paste, softened in
    1 teaspoon water
½ teaspoon *sambal ulek*
dash of tamarind juice
½ teaspoon salt
2 tablespoons margarine

Beat eggs slightly. Add scallion, shrimp paste, *sambel ulek*, tamarind juice and salt. Stir.

Heat margarine in frying pan. Pour in egg mixture and fry on both sides.

Cut into wide strips. Serve warm.

# Telur Dadar (Simple Omelette)

1 medium onion, chopped finely
1 medium red chilli, sliced thinly
1 tablespoon peanut oil
5 eggs
½ teaspoon salt
2 tablespoons margarine

Fry onion and chilli in peanut oil until earthy brown. Set aside.

Beat eggs slightly, add salt and prepare a regular omelette. As the omelette settles, sprinkle lightly with the onion-chilli combination, which gives the omelette a wonderful flavour. Turn the omelette over and do the same with the other side.

Cut into narrow strips and serve warm.

# Dadar Tegal (Omelette Tegal)

5 eggs
1 whole scallion, chopped coarsely
sliver of shrimp paste, softened in
   1 teaspoon water
½ teaspoon salt
2 tablespoons peanut oil

Beat eggs slightly. Add scallion, shrimp paste and salt, and stir.

Heat peanut oil in frying pan. Pour in egg mixture and fry on both sides.

Cut into broad strips and serve warm.

# Dadar Udang (Shrimp Omelette)

1 cup shelled fresh or frozen shrimps
1 tablespoon flour
3 tablespoons milk
6 eggs
pinch of nutmeg
pinch of pepper
1 teaspoon salt
3 tablespoons margarine
1 tablespoon parsley

Shell and devein shrimps. Chop fine.

Mix flour with milk.

Beat eggs slightly. Add batter to eggs and mix well. Then add nutmeg, pepper and salt, and stir. Add shrimp.

Make omelette in a large pan. Cut into broad strips, sprinkle with parsley and serve warm.

# Sambal Goreng Telur (Spiced Eggs)

*illustrated on page 88*

5 eggs, hard-boiled and sliced into halves
2 tablespoons peanut oil
1 medium onion, chopped
2 cloves garlic, chopped
1 candlenut, grated
1 teaspoon *laos*
1 teaspoon *sambal ulek*
salt to taste
½ teaspoon brown sugar
1 *salam* leaf
1 cup coconut milk from ½ coconut

Place the sliced eggs in a serving dish.

In separate pan, heat up peanut oil. Sauté onion, garlic, candlenut, *laos*, *sambal ulek* and salt. Be cautious to avoid burning.

Add brown sugar, *salam* leaf and coconut milk. Bring mixture to a boil and then simmer for 10 minutes.

Pour mixture over hard-boiled eggs and serve. Or, alternatively, place eggs in the spice mixture and heat together for a few minutes before serving.

# Telur Kari (Curried Eggs)

2 tablespoons peanut oil
1 medium onion, chopped
1 clove garlic, chopped
2 or more teaspoons curry powder
½ teaspoon lemon grass
1 teaspoon *sambal ulek*
1 *salam* leaf
1 lime leaf
1½ cups coconut milk from ½ coconut
1 teaspoon salt
6 eggs, hard-boiled

Heat peanut oil in a pan and add chopped onion and garlic. Add curry powder and mix well. Fry slightly.

Add lemon grass, *sambal ulek*, *salam* leaf, lime leaf, coconut milk and salt. Bring to a boil.

Add eggs and simmer for 10 minutes. Serve.

# Odds and Ends

Some Indonesian dishes defy classification, yet are integral parts of any rice table. Indeed, they are delicacies in themselves and are certain to whet the appreciative Western appetite. These dishes run the gamut from *krupuk* and *lumpia goreng* to *pisang goreng* and *bahmi*.

*Krupuk*, which is easily prepared, is a thin, lightweight, shrimp or fish wafer, somewhat similar to the American potato chip but made from a shrimp base. A *rijsttafel* is invariably garnished with a few *krupuk* crackers; so is almost any other Indonesian meal. On the cocktail circuit, perhaps needless to observe, they perform wonderfully as a titbit. Another favourite is *lumpia goreng*, a distant but discernible relative of the Chinese spring roll (erroneously but popularly called an egg roll by most Westerners). *Lumpia* is often served as an appetizer, accompanied by a ginger sauce. Most assuredly, Indonesia's version is Chinese in origin.

Another unclassified delight is *pisang goreng* or sautéed bananas prepared in the uncoated, West Indies style. The Indonesians also deep-fry them with a coating of flour and egg batter, as is the custom in South America. In Indonesia sautéed bananas should not be eaten during the meal. But in the colonial period, the Dutch considered a *rijsttafel* incomplete without sautéed bananas and the idea has gradually taken hold.

Europeanized hotels and restaurants now usually serve them with the main meal and the custom is spreading. Little wonder too, they contribute a marvellous flavour and act as a mild chutney in cooling the palate and providing a contrast to the hotly spiced side-dishes.

In this loose category of odds and ends, I have deliberately placed *bahmi* or noodle dishes, although purists will complain that they constitute a classification, if not a book, in themselves. I concede this point in Chinese or Vietnamese cookery but not when it comes to Indonesian, even though *bahmi*, which is an inexpensive, filling and nourishing dish, has assumed a prominent place in the average diet. Indonesian *bahmi* dishes are variations on a Chinese theme. They are not served at a rice table but constitute meals in themselves. Like Italian noodles, which Marco Polo introduced to Genoa after his return from Cathay, and the islands of silver (Sumatra) and gold (Java), *bahmi* comes in different lengths and widths. Several popular *bahmi* dishes follow in this section in recognition that a volume on Indonesian cooking would be incomplete without them, although *bahmi* is not an authentic Indonesian dish. Perhaps that statement is debatable. Is spaghetti an authentic Italian dish? The Italians would most assuredly claim it is.

# Krupuk Udang (Prawn Wafers)

*Melinjo wafers — Emping, has the consistency of prawn wafers and is white in appearance. The wafer is the roasted fruit of the tropical melinjo tree and has a delightful taste, almost like burnt almond. It is cooked in the same fashion as prawn wafers but sprinkled with salt before serving.*

**2 cups vegetable oil**
**2 dozen uncooked prawn wafers**

Bring vegetable oil to a boil in a heavy frying pan.

Fry the wafers singly. In the frying process, the dainty wafers will treble in size. Stir continuously during frying and remove from pan with slotted turner.

Place the wafers on absorbent paper towelling. Serve hot or cold as desired.

# Rempeyeh (Peanut Fritter)

**1 cup rice flour**
**1 cup coconut milk**
**½ teaspoon coriander**
**½ teaspoon salt**
**1 clove garlic, chopped**
**pinch of cummin**
**pinch of turmeric**
**1 candlenut, grated**
**½ cup raw peanuts**
**oil for deep-frying**

Mix rice flour with coconut milk. Then add coriander, salt, garlic, cummin, turmeric and candlenut. Mix well.

Now add the raw peanuts. The batter will be on the watery side.

Heat oil, and fry batter by the tablespoon. Fry until golden brown. Drain on absorbent paper. Serve.

The Rempeyeh will be like a flat thin cooky.

# Rempah Kelapa (Spicy Coconut Balls)

*illustrated on page 26*

1 cup coconut, desiccated or freshly grated
2 cloves garlic, chopped
2 eggs
1 tablespoon flour
1 tablespoon tamarind juice
½ teaspoon lemon grass
½ teaspoon coriander
½ teaspoon *laos*
pinch of turmeric
pinch of sugar
1 *salam* leaf, crushed
sliver of shrimp paste
1 teaspoon salt
vegetable oil for deep-frying

With the exception of oil, mix all ingredients thoroughly in a bowl. Fashion tiny balls from the resulting mixture, about the size of pigeon eggs.

Heat vegetable oil to boiling point and deep-fry several balls at a time until deep brown. To be served as a *rijsttafel* garnish.

# Serundeng (Coconut-peanut Garnish)

1 tablespoon vegetable oil
1 medium onion, sliced
3 cloves garlic, chopped
½ teaspoon coriander
pinch of cummin
½ teaspoon *laos*
¼ roll shrimp paste
1 teaspoon brown sugar
1 *salam* leaf
1 teaspoon salt
1 cup coconut, desiccated or freshly grated
½ cup roasted peanuts, salted or unsalted

Heat vegetable oil in an iron skillet. Add onion and garlic. Sauté lightly and then add coriander, cummin, *laos*, shrimp paste, brown sugar, *salam* leaf and salt. Stir well and keep heat low.

Add coconut and toast ingredients, stirring continuously until coconut turns an even, crisp, medium brown.

Now mix in the roasted peanuts and fry for about 3 minutes. Remove from heat, cool and serve as *rijsttafel* garnish.

# Bahmi Goreng sama Udang
# (Shrimp and Noodles)

1 lb (450 g) medium egg noodles
1 lb (450 g) shelled fresh shrimps
2 tablespoons vegetable oil
1 medium onion, sliced
2 cloves garlic, chopped
1 tablespoon light soy sauce
1 bouillon chicken cube, dissolved in
   1 cup hot water
3 whole scallions, cut thinly

Bring water to a boil. Put in noodles and cook for 1 minute until tender. Then run under cold tap water and drain with strainer.

Separately in a heavy skillet, fry shrimps in vegetable oil for about 5 minutes. Add onion and garlic to shrimps and fry mixture until onion slices turn medium brown.

Then add soy sauce and cooked noodles, mixing thoroughly.

Add a small amount of bouillon to noodle mixture to prevent burning and pan-sticking.

Finally mix scallions with noodles. Fry until dry but avoid burning. Serve in an oval-shaped platter.

This dish constitutes a meal in itself and can be garnished with a plain omelette sliced into thin strips, and with parsley.

# Bahmi Goreng Ayam (Chicken and Noodles)

½ lb (225 g) medium egg noodles
1 chicken breast
3 cloves garlic, chopped
3 tablespoons vegetable oil
1 tablespoon soy sauce, light or dark
3 cabbage leaves, cut thinly
salt to taste
1 scallion, sliced
½ lb (225 g) shelled cooked shrimps

Bring water to a boil, then put in noodles to cook for 1 minute until tender. Run under cold tap water, and drain with strainer. Set aside.

Separately, remove meat from chicken breast and dice. Lightly fry chicken and garlic in vegetable oil in a heavy skillet. Add soy sauce,

stir well and fry an additional minute.

Add cabbage and fry until cabbage appears to wilt.

Now add cooked noodles and salt to taste. Stir continuously, cooking over low heat.

Add scallion and fry for about 2 minutes.

Mix in cooked shrimps and heat whole mixture for another 2 minutes, again stirring frequently. Serve on an oval platter. May be garnished with a plain omelette or fried onion.

*Note:* Bahmi Goreng Babi (Pork and Noodles) and Bahmi Goreng Sapi (Beef and Noodles) may be cooked in the same manner using pork and beef instead of chicken. It is also common to mix chicken, pork, shrimps and crab meat together in any combination.

# Lumpia Goreng (Indonesian Egg Rolls)

*illustrated on page 106*

*This dish requires 3 separate stages of preparation, to wit: 1) the filling 2) the wrapping and 3) the sauce. In Indonesia Lumpia Goreng is often served as an appetizer, while in the West it also makes a fine cocktail snack.*

### Stage 1: The Filling

1 small chicken breast
2 tablespoons vegetable oil
½ cup shelled fresh shrimps
2 cloves garlic, chopped
1 tablespoon sweet soy sauce
3 white, inner cabbage leaves
1 cup bean sprouts
2 whole scallions, chopped
salt to taste

Remove meat from chicken breast and dice. Fry chicken in vegetable oil in a heavy skillet for about 5 minutes.

Dice shrimps and add to skillet. Now fry 3 additional minutes.

Add garlic and fry until garlic turns light brown. Add soy sauce and stir well.

Shred cabbage leaves finely and add to mixture, again stirring well. Add bean sprouts and mix thoroughly into the mixture.

Finally add scallion to other ingredients and put over low heat for a few minutes until cabbage appears slightly wilted. Set aside and cool completely. While filling is cooling, prepare the wrapping.

### Stage 2: The Wrapping

1 egg
2 tablespoons margarine
½ teaspoon salt
1 cup flour
oil for deep-frying

Beat egg slightly and add melted margarine. Stir well and add salt.

Now mix in flour as though making a pie crust. Add just enough water to make a dough.

Then drop a tablespoon of dough at a time on a floured board and roll out as thinly as possible. The pastry wrapping is now ready for filling.

Fill each piece of dough with cooked mixture, fold the ends and seal with water or beaten egg white.

Deep-fry until light brown. Serve with either hot English mustard or the following ginger sauce.

### Stage 3: The Sauce

½ teaspoon *sambal ulek*
pinch of chopped ginger
1 teaspoon sugar
1 teaspoon cornstarch
1 teaspoon dark soy sauce
1 tablespoon tamarind juice
3 tablespoons water

Mix all ingredients together in a small enamel saucepan. Stir thoroughly and put over low heat until sauce thickens. Serve.

*Note:* A shorter and simpler method would be to mix together 4 tablespoons apricot jam, a pinch of chopped ginger and 2 tablespoons soy sauce.

# Condiments

In the realm of condiments, the unbridled Indonesian imagination runs riot. Dozens of variations on a theme may appear on the rice table simultaneously. At this point the problem for the hostess is to possess not one, but several lazy susans.

The variety of condiments available in the Indonesian islands puts to shame the appearance on the Western table of the standard salt and pepper shakers, Maggi or, in the case of the American, the ubiquitous ketchup bottle (sometimes spelt 'catsup'). The word 'ketchup', incidentally, is derived from the Malay word for soy sauce, *kecap.* In the West, of course, ketchup is wholly made from tomatoes.

Perhaps the most imaginative Indonesian garnish is *garam dan marica,* simply salt and pepper mixed together and served in a small dish instead of a shaker. Try it sometime, and not necessarily with Indonesian food. In Jakarta, and elsewhere in the archipelago, Chinese restaurants invariably serve this mixture with frog legs fried in butter. It makes for a magnificent snack and should be washed down with cold beer.

Western condiments are generally bland compared to the condiments found in the archipelago. To the uninitiated, the indiscriminate use of *sambals* will bring tears to the eyes and a burst of perspiration to the brow. Sometimes, though rarely, it even causes the initiated to cry — with joy, however.

As in the case of spices, not all Indonesian condiments or *sambals* are fiery hot. Several — particularly those involving the preparation of cucumbers, which may be served sliced and raw — are designed to cool the palate. These condiments assay a role similar to that of chutney in Indian cooking.

The preparation of *sambals* is complex, but fortunately the growing popularity of Indonesian cooking has provided the cook with a short cut. Outside Southeast Asia, *sambals* may be purchased either from importers of foreign foods or directly from Holland. The biggest company in the Netherlands handling this and other Indonesian foods is Conimex. It is located at Baarn, the Netherlands.

*Sambals* are relatively inexpensive and come in small bottles. They are used sparingly with a meal. So do not let the profusion of different *sambals* frighten you. There are six basic ones, as follows:

*sambal ulek,* a fiery, crushed red chilli mixture whose thermostat has been raised by the addition of other hot spices.
*sambal manis,* a mild, sweet-tasting condiment.
*sambal goreng,* a popular blend of red chilli and other spices but dissimilar to *sambal ulek.*
*sambal udang kering,* a condiment made from shrimp paste, a form commonly found in Thailand, Burma, Cambodia and, of course, Malaysia.
*sambal peteh,* a condiment made from the *peteh* bean which has an unusually strong and unpleasant odour, but which has a rare and tantalizing taste.
*sambal bajak,* a fiery condiment which has a dull taste — and a delayed reaction.

Each of these *sambals* is used in the course of a *rijsttafel,* a dash at a time. Customarily, they

A selection of Indonesian condiments and relishes

Lumpia Goreng (p. 103)

Buah-buah Amandel (p. 121) with Serikaya (p. 122)

Pisang Goreng and Nanas Goreng (p. 121)

are served either in a small dish or in the original bottle with a tiny spoon.

The *sambals* develop taste sensations wholly absent from Chinese, Western and Indian cookery.

Several types of *sambals,* however, can be easily prepared in the modern kitchen, requiring little more than a few spices and some cucumber, lemon, onion or coconut. The following recipes belong to this group. You will find that these relishes provide a new dimension to your adventures in eating.

# Sambal Kecap (Spiced Soya)

2 long red chillies
3 tablespoons dark soy sauce

Slice chillies into elongated strips and float in soy sauce. Serve in condiment dish. Especially good with chicken dishes and all kinds of satay.

# Sambal Kelapa (Spicy Coconut)

3 tablespoons coconut, desiccated or freshly grated
1 green chilli, crushed
sliver of shrimp paste
½ teaspoon *laos*
½ teaspoon salt
1 tablespoon vegetable oil

Sauté all ingredients in vegetable oil over medium heat, stirring constantly, until coconut appears to be turning light brown. Serve.

# Sambal Jelantah (Spiced Chillies with Shrimp Paste)

4 red chillies, chopped finely
4 green chillies, chopped finely
1 teaspoon shrimp paste
½ teaspoon salt
1 tablespoon vegetable oil

Sauté chillies, shrimp paste and salt in vegetable oil for about 2 minutes.

Add 4 tablespoons water and simmer on low heat until liquid is halved. Serve in condiment dish.

*Note:* If fresh chillies are not available, dried crushed chillies may be substituted.

# Sambal Jeruk (Spicy Lemon)

1 lemon
2 red chillies, crushed
sliver of shrimp paste
1 teaspoon salt

Cut lemon into wafer-thin slices. Place in serving bowl and add chillies, shrimp paste and salt. Mix thoroughly. Serve.

# Sambal Ketimun (Spicy Cucumber)

1 large cucumber
2 candlenuts, grated
2 red chillies, crushed
sliver of shrimp paste
¼ cup vinegar
½ teaspoon salt

Peel and slice cucumber into thin strips and set aside.

Separately, place candlenuts in a bowl and add chillies, shrimp paste, vinegar, ¼ cup water and salt. Stir well.

Now float cucumber strips in mixture and serve.

Spicy Cucumber is an important *rijsttafel* dish, for it cools and soothes the palate.

# Sambal Ulek (Chillies and Spices)

*This mixture is an ingredient in most Indonesian dishes. It can be kept in the refrigerator for several weeks.*

1 dozen red chillies
½ teaspoon shrimp paste
½ teaspoon salt
1 tablespoon tamarind juice

Pound chillies, shrimp paste and salt together in a mortar. Stir in tamarind juice.

A simpler method would be to mix all ingredients in an electric blender.

# Sambal Bajak (Fried Spicy Chillies)

1 medium onion, chopped finely
6 cloves garlic, chopped finely
1 tablespoon vegetable oil
3 red chillies, crushed
1 teaspoon salt
1 tablespoon brown sugar
12 candlenuts, grated
½ teaspoon *laos*
1 teaspoon shrimp paste
2 *salam* leaves
1 lemon grass leaf
2 lime leaves
1 tablespoon tamarind juice

Sauté onion and garlic in vegetable oil until light brown.

Add chillies, salt and brown sugar. Fry mixture for about 2 minutes.

Now combine with the rest of the ingredients. Stir well, fry several minutes and add 6 tablespoons of water.

Simmer over low heat until almost dry. Place in a jar after removing leaves. It can be kept for a very long period.

# Relishes

No *rijsttafel,* nor for that matter Asian dinner, is complete without an array of relishes and/or pickles. Relishes, like the tributaries of a river, feed the mainstream. They add zest to any dinner and 'zest', according to both the Oxford and Webster dictionaries, is something which enhances a pleasant taste. Coincidentally, of course, the relish imparts a taste of its own.

In the West, relishes are normally piquant. In Southeast Asia, they run the gamut searingly spicy to pungent sweet. In the islands, however, *acars* or relishes are invariably mild. They tend to complement the hot dishes prepared with *sambal goreng. Acars* alert the palate for the next round.

Indonesia's relishes are different and easy to prepare. They are often made several days in advance and may be stored for a considerable length of time under routine refrigeration. With an Indonesian meal, *acars* are a must. In the West, they are ideally suited to barbecues, with either American-style hamburgers or broiled steaks. One of the most popular brands of *acar* in Indonesia, a sort of household Heinz, is Mevr Kouw, a superb Sino-Indonesian mixture of pickled cauliflower, cucumbers, dill and so forth.

# Ketimun (Cucumber)

2 large cucumbers

Peel cucumbers and then cut them in half. Remove pulp and slice into elongated strips. Serve this cold as an accompaniment to the spicy-hot main courses.

# Acar Ketimun (Pickled Cucumber)

1 large cucumber
2 teaspoons vinegar
1 teaspoon salt
1 red chilli, crushed

Peel cucumber and cut into thin circular slices. Place in serving bowl and set aside.

Now mix vinegar, ½ cup water and salt in a bowl. Float cucumber in liquid and sprinkle with chillies. Serve with rice dishes.

# Acar Ketimun Jawa (Javanese Pickled Cucumber)

1 large cucumber
2 teaspoons salt
⅓ cup vinegar
¼ cup granulated sugar
3 peppercorns
3 whole cloves

Cube cucumber into bite-size portions and place in earthen pot. Set aside.

Now mix salt, ¼ cup water, vinegar, sugar, peppercorns and cloves in saucepan and bring to a slow boil.

Lower heat and simmer another 5 minutes.

Pour liquid over cucumber. Cool in earthen pot. Stand for 3 days before serving.

# Acar Ketimun Kuning
# (Yellow Pickled Cucumbers)

3 large cucumbers
1 small onion, chopped finely
¼ cup vinegar
¼ cup granulated sugar
2 whole cloves
pinch of chopped ginger
1 teaspoon ground turmeric
2 teaspoons salt

Peel cucumbers and slice lengthwise. Remove pulp and slice into bite-size portions. Place in a pyrex dish and set aside.

Place onion in saucepan and add ⅓ cup water, vinegar, sugar, cloves, ginger, turmeric and salt. Bring to a boil and simmer for 15 minutes.

Pour liquid over cucumber. Cool and cover. Refrigerate for at least 4 hours before serving. Serve cold.

# Acar Bawang Pedes (Spicy Pickled Onion)

1 large onion, chopped finely
4 tablespoons tamarind juice
2 teaspoons hot pepper sauce

Mix all 3 ingredients together and serve.

# Acar Nanas (Pickled Pineapple)

1 small pineapple
whole cloves
½ cup vinegar
¼ cup sugar

Peel pineapple and remove core. Cut into serving portions. Tack a nail-shaped clove into each piece of pineapple. Place in an earthen bean pot.

Meanwhile, in a saucepan, bring to a slow boil a mixture of vinegar, sugar and ⅔ cup water. Simmer for 10 minutes.

Pour the liquid over the pineapple. Cool. Cover and pickle for at least 6 hours. Serve.

# Acar Biet (Pickled Beets)

4 beets
3 whole cloves
3 peppercorns
1 tablespoon brown sugar
⅓ cup vinegar

Boil beets, peel and cut into slices.

In a separate pot, boil the remaining ingredients in ⅓ cup water. Simmer for 15 minutes.

Marinate beets in solution for at least 2 hours. Serve.

# Acar Bloemkool (Pickled Cauliflower)

1 small head cauliflower
½ teaspoon turmeric
pinch of chopped ginger
¼ cup vinegar
1 clove garlic
1 tablespoon granulated sugar
1 teaspoon salt

Gently dismember the cauliflower head and make florets. Parboil florets and drain.

Now boil separately turmeric, ginger, vinegar, garlic, ⅓ cup water, sugar and salt. Pour the resulting liquid over cauliflower.

Stand in a covered dish for at least 12 hours. Serve cool.

# Acar Campur (Mixed Pickles)

½ lb (225 g) cabbage, sliced into strips
½ lb (225 g) string beans, sliced into strips
1 carrot, sliced into strips
1 teaspoon turmeric
1½ tablespoons sugar
⅓ cup vinegar
2 teaspoons salt

Parboil the sliced vegetables, and then drain.

Separately, bring turmeric, sugar, vinegar, ⅔ cup water and salt to a boil. Pour liquid over mixed vegetables.

Cover and let stand for at least 6 hours before serving.

# Acar Campur Ulek (Spicy Mixed Pickles)

½ head cabbage, chopped finely making 2 cups
½ lb (225 g) string beans, chopped finely
1 carrot, chopped finely
2 candlenuts, grated
2 tablespoons vegetable oil
1 medium onion
1 teaspoon *sambal ulek*
⅓ cup vinegar
⅔ teaspoon salt

Melt vegetable oil in a pan and sauté onion, *sambal ulek* and candlenuts together.

Now add ½ cup water, vinegar and salt, and bring to a slow boil.

Add vegetables and cook until tender. Cool, then serve.

# Acar Buncis (Pickled String Beans)

1 lb (450 g) string beans, with strings removed
3 whole cloves
3 peppercorns
½ teaspoon *sambal ulek*
1 tablespoon granulated sugar
2 teaspoons salt
½ cup vinegar

Pack string beans upright in a mason or pyrex jar. Add cloves, peppercorns and *sambal ulek*.

Separately, bring ½ cup water, sugar, salt and vinegar to a boil. Simmer for about 10 minutes. Pour liquid over the beans.

Seal the jar. Stand for at least 3 days before serving.

# Acar Bawang Timor (Pickled Onions)

1 dozen small white onions
3 candlenuts, grated
1 teaspoon oil
pinch of ginger
pinch of turmeric
½ cup vinegar
1 teaspoon salt

Peel onions, then wash and dry them with absorbent paper towels. Place the onions in earthen bean pot or a glass jar.

Heat oil in a pan and sauté candlenuts, ginger and turmeric lightly. Add vinegar, 1 cup water and salt.

Bring to a boil and then simmer for 10 to 15 minutes. Pour liquid over onions. Cool. Cover and let it stand for at least 5 days before serving.

# Rujak Buah-buah Pedes
## (Hot Fruit Chutney)

2 tart apples or green mangoes
2 hard, green pears
1 teaspoon sugar
1 teaspoon sweet soy sauce
1 tablespoon tamarind juice
1 teaspoon *sambal ulek*

Peel fruit and cut into medium-thick slices. Separately, mix sugar, soy sauce, tamarind juice and *sambal ulek*.

Add fruit and stir thoroughly. Serve.

# Rujak Sayur Pedes
## (Spicy Vegetable Chutney)

2 firm tomatoes, peeled and quartered
1 small cucumber, peeled and diced
2 radishes, sliced
1 teaspoon sweet soy sauce
2 tablespoons vinegar
½ teaspoon salt
2 teaspoons brown sugar
1 teaspoon *sambal ulek*
sliver of shrimp paste

Mix soy sauce, vinegar, salt, brown sugar, *sambal ulek* and shrimp paste.

Add vegetables and stir well. Serve.

# Desserts

Indonesian buffet-luncheons or dinners, that is, *rijsttafel,* invariably end with a bowl of fresh fruit. Little wonder: there simply is no place for rich desserts. This is not to suggest that the islanders do not like sweets. Indonesians usually restrict their intake of rich, glazed cakes to either festive occasions or coffee-tea breaks.

Sometimes a *rijsttafel* is concluded with bananas lightly fried in coconut oil or margarine, or perhaps a pancake made from rice flour and filled with grated coconut and palm sugar or caramelized sugar. The fried banana is often served with the rice table itself.

In the big Indonesian seaports and towns, such Western concoctions as ice cream or sherbets are also popular desserts.

Perhaps the principal reason why Indonesians place such emphasis on fresh fruits is their natural abundance in most of the islands. Their variety is staggering, even when compared to the rest of Southeast Asia. The banana, for example, comes in any number of varieties. Among the most popular is the *pisang Ambon* or Ambonese banana, which resembles the Central American variety, invariably found in European and North American supermarkets. Then there is the *pisang batu* or stone banana which is pitted with tiny, granite-like seeds or stones. The lady-finger banana (also called gold banana or *pisang emas*) which is, as the name suggests, about the length of a lady's finger, is a delight. By contrast in size, there is the *pisang panjang* or long banana which is a foot in length. Perhaps the sweetest to the taste is the *pisang susu* or milk banana. Among the bananas there is also the *pisang raja,* which as its name implies, is the king of bananas.

Similarly, the islanders do not have one kind of pineapple, but many varieties. And the wide-ranging number of *jeruks* or citrus fruits found in Indonesia is stunning. Indeed, the common grapefruit and many other citrus fruits grown around the world are native to the archipelago. Sometimes the size is startling, if not staggering. The *jeruk Bali* or pomelo is a case in point. It is the size of a coconut. Then, of course, there is an array of papaya and mangoes (although the Indian mango, particularly from around Cochin has, I believe, a better taste). But these are fairly pedestrian fruits, known the world wide.

What makes Indonesian fruit spectacular is the fantastic variety (some of which defy description, and which have no colloquial Western names), such as the mangosteen, rambutan, durian, kedong-dong, belimbing, sawa, duku-duku, jambu, nangka, salak and so forth. Many of these are found in the market-places of Southeast Asia, notably in Singapore, Bangkok, Kuala Lumpur and Rangoon. With the exception of the nangka, which is similar to the jackfruit of central America, the others are not only unknown outside the region, but are beyond imagination.

Take the first three I mentioned, for example. The mangosteen has been universally acclaimed by travellers from China and the West as the 'queen of fruits'. It has been compared by the Dutch plantologist, Jacobus Bontius, to nectar and ambrosia. It has been said to surpass the taste of the golden apples of the Hesperides. Indeed, one American botanist concluded: 'It is doubtful whether the world possesses another tropical fruit which is its equal.' Yet in the Indonesian islands, the mangosteen grows wild. It can be found growing in almost every village. The fruit is the size of an apple, has a vivid, purple skin and a translucent pulp of indescribable deliciousness. Mangosteen combines the flavour of the nectarine peach and palm, to develop an hypnotic sensation of its own. In season, it is commonly served at the end of a *rijsttafel,* together with a multitude of desserts.

The second fruit on the list is the rambutan (in Malay, *rambut* means hair). About the size of a lemon, the rambutan is usually red in colour, sometimes greenish-yellow. It is covered with ugly, unappetizing hairs. But the shell is soft and can be easily split with a fingernail, exposing a juicy, acidulous, white mass. Probably the closest fruit to a rambutan is the Chinese *litchi* or spring plum. The first Westerner who stumbled on the rambutan was a Frenchman who immediately dubbed it *litchi chevelu* — the hairy *litchi.*

*Litchi,* incidentally, make an excellent climax to a *rijsttafel* and can be obtained these days as easily in England or Australia as anywhere else. They are invariably tinned in Canton, Taiwan or Hong Kong. Writing about the *litchi* always vividly brings to mind the finest I have ever eaten. It was in 1949, when my husband and I joined the Chokorda, Agung Gede Agung Sukawati, at Ubud, Bali, under a *litchi* tree. We spent the better part of the day leaning against the tree, chatting aimlessly and munching on the fresh fruit swinging gently above our heads. After two or three hours, a small European car flashed by the village and the Chokorda seemed troubled. 'Bali is becoming so hasty', he sighed. The last time I saw the Chokorda at Ubud was in 1954. By then, tourism had regained some of its pre-war lustre and I counted eight cars passing through in a single day. The din was dreadful.

No commentary on Indonesia's fruit is complete without a reference to the third variety on the impoverished list above. This is the controversial durian. Either you like it or you do not. Unlike the olive, a taste for it cannot be acquired. The best I have ever eaten were on the island of Borneo. It is, perhaps, the only tropical fruit which can rival the mangosteen, although in appearance and taste they are completely dissimilar.

It is fitting to quote a European traveller in Java, in 1599. Of the durian, he wrote: 'The durian is about the size of a pineapple. Its pulp is like mellow custard.' Since then many writers have attempted to describe its taste, but none have succeeded. The most glowing report was produced by Alfred Russel Wallace who, with Charles Darwin, shares the theory on the origin of species and whose monumental work, *The Malay Archipelago,* is a treasure-trove of information about the islands. In the opinion of this English naturalist, the durian tastes like 'rich, butter-like custard highly flavoured with almonds.' This, however, he confessed, only gives a general idea of its taste. 'But intermingled with it comes wafts of flavour that call to mind cream cheese, onion sauce, brown sherry and other incongruities,' he said. 'It is neither acid nor sweet, nor juicy, yet one feels the want of none of these qualities for it is perfect as it is. In fact, to eat durian is a new sensation, worth a voyage to the East to experience.'

Nature has provided the durian with greater protection than that possibly enjoyed by any other fruit. Its outer skin is coarse. It is also spiked. And for additional protection nature has provided it with a rancid, putrid, vile, disagreeable, incredibly bad odour. The late, unlamented Sukarno regime served it on a state menu for a visiting VIP, Khrushchev. This was in 1960 and caused one correspondent to term it the first publicized confrontation between Soviet man and the durian.

These few paragraphs provide only a hint of the variety of fruit found in the Indonesian archipelago, indeed, in the Malay world. It also explains why the *rijsttafel* often ends on a fruity note. The suggestion then is that you end your rice table or buffet with a basket of fruit. Use whatever is at hand, whether tropical or cold-weather fruits such as cherries, pears, apples, grapes and so forth. A dish of ice cream is also a superb climax to a *rijsttafel.*

# Pisang Goreng (Banana Fritters)

*illustrated on page 108*

**2 eggs**
**6 tablespoons flour**
**2 ripe bananas**
**oil for deep-frying**
**cinnamon sugar**

Slightly beat eggs and mix with flour and ½ cup water.

Mash bananas with a fork and mix thoroughly with flour and egg mixture. Deep-fry banana and flour mixture by the tablespoonful in hot oil until golden brown.

Drain on absorbent paper and dust with cinnamon sugar.

*Note:* If you substitute thinly sliced pineapple for the banana, you come up with Nanas Goreng (Pineapple Fritters).

# Buah-buah Amandel (Almond Delight)

*illustrated on page 107*

**1 cup milk**
**4 tablespoons sugar**
**1 envelope unflavoured gelatin (or sufficient agar-agar to gel 2 cups of liquid)**
**1 tablespoon or more almond extract**
**1 can tinned fruit, such as litchi, mandarin orange, rambutan or fruit cocktail**

In a small pot, bring milk, 1 cup water and sugar to a fast boil. Turn off heat. With a fork, beat unflavoured gelatin into the mixture. Pour cooked mixture into a dish.

After the mixture has been allowed to stand and cool slightly, add almond extract and mix well. Cover and refrigerate overnight.

To serve, pour your choice of tinned fruit over the almond jelly, including the syrup. Though any kind can be used, mandarin orange goes well as the snowy white and orange make a lovely combination.

# Serikaya (Coconut Custard)

*illustrated on page 107*

**4 eggs**
**6 tablespoons white sugar**
**2 cups coconut milk**
**brown sugar or *gula Jawa***

Beat eggs and white sugar together until sugar is dissolved. Mix with coconut milk.

Line individual cups (pyrex, for instance) with a bit of brown sugar or a piece of *gula Jawa*. Pour the coconut mixture into cups until full.

Place the cups in a pan of water and steam until cooked. Test with a toothpick or knife in the centre. If it comes out clean it is done.

Allow to cool and then place in the refrigerator.

Before serving dip a knife in hot water and loosen the edges. Place a serving dish on top and turn the coconut custard upside down. It should pop right out.

*Note:* This dish can also be made in a single large pie dish.

# Fried Bananas Flambé

**bananas**
**margarine**
**Cointreau, Grand Marnier, rum or cognac**

Peel bananas and sauté them whole in a teflon pan in margarine.

Place on a serving dish.

Pour over a few tablespoonfuls of Cointreau, Grand Marnier, rum or cognac. Light a match, and watch the blue flame flicker away — a truly spectacular sight, and tastes great as well.

*Note:* In the United States and Europe large bananas are likely to be available. Peel them and slice them in half before sautéeing.

# Ingredient Substitutes

Some common Western items make ideal substitutes for Indonesian ingredients. Indeed, in some instances the application of Indonesian cooking methods provides the Western-prepared product with a refreshing lilt.

| Indonesian ingredient | Substitute |
|---|---|
| banana leaves | aluminium foil *or* husk of fresh ear of corn |
| *batu garam* | coarse salt (kosher) |
| chilli | red pepper |
| coconut milk | homogenized milk |
| ground peanuts | peanut butter |
| *gula Jawa* | brown sugar |
| *gula Melaka* | see *gula Jawa* |
| *kacang panjang* | asparagus beans |
| *kakap* or *gurami* | sea bass *or* porgy |
| *kangkong* | watercress |
| *kemerie* nuts | Hawaiian macadamia nuts |
| rice flour | cream of rice |
| *salam* leaves | bay *or* laurel leaves |
| *sambal ulek* | Italian-style crushed red pepper |
| small red onions | common white onion |
| sweet soy sauce | equal amounts of Chinese *or* Japanese soy sauce and molasses |
| tamarind juice | lemon juice |
| *trassi* | anchovy paste |

# Some Suggested Menus

(for 4—6 persons depending on appetites)

**Menu 1**

Rice
Sambal Goreng Kool
Ayam Kecap
Krupuk
Acars
Fruit

**Menu 2**

Bahmi Goreng
Satay (any kind)
Krupuk or emping
Sherbet or ice cream

**Menu 3**

Nasi Kuning
Ayam Panggang
Acars
Sambal Bajak
Krupuk
Fruit

**Menu 4**

Rice
Rendang Padang
Corn Croquettes
Soy Fish
Krupuk
Assorted sambals
Dessert

By adding 1 more dish every time the hostess can feed at least 2 more guests.

Since there is no stir-frying involved as in Chinese cooking, the cook has more leisure. The only last-minute preparation would be in the satay.

Krupuk, emping, etc., can be fried the day before and kept in air-tight containers. Pickles can be made ahead of time also.

# Kitchen Glossary

| Indonesian | English |
|---|---|
| abu | ash |
| abu-abu (tonny) | tuna |
| acar | pickles |
| agar-agar | gelatin |
| air | water |
| air-Belanda | soda water |
| akar | root |
| anggur | wine |
| angin | wind |
| api | fire |
| arak | liquor from rice wine |
| arang | charcoal |
| asam | sour; tamarind |
| asin | salted |
| ayam | chicken |
| babi | pig; pork |
| bahmi | noodles |
| bakar | roast; grill |
| bandeng | an Indonesian fish |
| banjar | mackerel |
| banteng | buffalo |
| bantu | help |

| Indonesian | English |
| --- | --- |
| banyak | much |
| baru | new; fresh |
| bawang | onion |
| bawang putih | garlic |
| bayem | spinach |
| bebek | duck |
| begedel | croquettes |
| Belanda | Dutch |
| beras | uncooked rice |
| berguling | roast on a spit |
| biet | beet |
| bieting | wooden sticks or skewers |
| biji | grain; seed; pit |
| blacan | shrimp paste |
| bloemkool | cauliflower |
| buah | fruit |
| bubur | porridge |
| bumbu | spices |
| buncis | string bean |
| burung darah | pigeon |
| cakalang | bonito |
| campur | mixed |
| cuka | vinegar |
| dadar | omelette |
| daging | meat |
| dapur | kitchen |
| daun | leaf |
| daun salam | Java laurel leaf |

| Indonesian | English |
| --- | --- |
| dendeng | dried, spicy meat |
| dingin | cold |
| durian | a fruit |
| emping | vegetable wafer |
| es | ice |
| es krim | ice cream |
| gado-gado | mixed cooked vegetables |
| garam | salt |
| garpu | fork |
| gemuk | fat |
| goreng | fry |
| gula | sugar |
| gurami | carp |
| guri | fragrant |
| hati | liver |
| hijau | green |
| ikan | fish |
| ikan emas | gold fish, carp |
| ikan kakaktua | parrot fish, similar to black fish |
| ikan lajar | sail fish |
| ikan teri | anchovy |
| istimewa | special |
| jagung | corn |
| jahe | ginger |
| jeruk | citrus |
| jintan | cummin |
| kacang | bean; nut; peanut |
| kacang kapri | peas |

| Indonesian | English |
| --- | --- |
| kacang panjang | oriental long bean |
| kacang tanah | peanut |
| kakap | Indonesian sea perch |
| kambing | goat |
| kari | curry |
| kecap | soy sauce |
| kelapa | coconut |
| kembang | flower |
| kemerie | candlenut |
| kembang pala | mace |
| kencur | ginger-like root |
| kepiting | crab; lobster |
| ketimun | cucumber |
| ketumbar | coriander |
| kipas | fan (for outdoor grill) |
| kodok | frog |
| kool | cabbage |
| krupuk | shrimp or meat wafer |
| kucai | leek |
| kuning | yellow |
| kunyit | turmeric |
| kuro | barracuda |
| lajang | jackfish |
| langkau | halibut |
| laos (lengkuas) | a spice root |
| laut | sea |
| lemuru | sardine |
| lombok | type of hot pepper |

| Indonesian | English |
| --- | --- |
| makan | eat |
| makanan | food |
| manis | sweet |
| manisan | sweets |
| masak | to cook |
| mata sapi | fried egg (sunny-side up) |
| meja | table |
| mengiris | to slice finely |
| mentega | butter |
| merica | pepper |
| minyak | oil |
| nanas | pineapple |
| nasi | rice |
| otak | sweet breads; brains |
| padi | rice plant; unhusked rice |
| pala | nutmeg |
| panggang | roasting; grilling |
| pare-pare | bitter gourd |
| pasar | market |
| pedes | spicy; hot |
| penyu | turtle |
| pisang | banana |
| pisau | knife |
| potong | to cut |
| prei | leeks |
| rebung | bamboo shoot |
| rebus | boiled |
| rempah | spice mixtures |

| Indonesian | English |
| --- | --- |
| roti | bread |
| sambal | hot sauce mixtures |
| sambalan | spiced dishes |
| santan-santan | coconut milk |
| sapi | cow; beef |
| satay | grilled meat on skewers |
| saus | sauce |
| sawi | mustard greens |
| sayur | vegetables |
| sereh | lemon grass |
| serundeng | fried, grated spicy coconut |
| sop | soup |
| susu | milk |
| tahu | bean cake |
| taugeh | bean sprouts |
| telur | eggs |
| tepung | flour |
| tepung beras | rice flour |
| terung | eggplant; brinjal |
| toko | store; shop |
| tomat | tomato |
| trassi | shrimp paste |
| tuak | palm wine |
| tulang | bone |
| udang | shrimp |
| wajan | Indonesian frying pan |
| wortel | carrots |